Also by Carla Da Costa

*Seconds Please: Lessons on life, love and
self after divorce*

Finding Love After Divorce

How to know if they're the one
or just another one

Finding Love After Divorce

CARLA DA COSTA

A catalogue record for this book is available from the National Library of Australia.

Trade Paperback ISBN: 978-0-6455978-9-9
eBook ISBN: 978-0-6455978-8-2

Print information available on the last page.

The kind press acknowledges Australia's First Nations peoples as the traditional owners and custodians of this country, and we pay our respects to their elders, past and present.

THE
KIND
PRESS

www.thekindpress.com

CONTENTS

Preface

The one.

Do we just have one 'one'?

Or do we have many?

Maybe you believe in 'the one', maybe you don't. Certainly, in my own personal journey since my divorce, I have been in relationships where I thought they were the one and my happily-ever-after. Until I realised they were not. Hindsight and heartbreak are humbling like that.

The one goes on to sometimes disappoint us so badly that we look back on them and wonder how we could have ever been so blind to who they really were. Realising that what we believed was a good fit was more us wishing it so.

They never really deserved the pedestal we had placed them on. Or we begin to look at them over time and recognise that our feelings have changed. Yes, we still have love for them, but it's different. Love for them more like a brother or a sister. A friend, even.

These loves can often be the hardest to let go of. We love them but we're 'not in love' with them. The heartbreak that someone goes through after a partner leaves them is often talked about. What's rarely discussed is the inner turmoil and pain someone experienced in the years leading up to asking their partner for a divorce. This person didn't necessarily want to separate or hurt anyone's feelings. They just couldn't keep pretending and living a lie anymore.

Love is unique like that. It transcends all rational understanding. It's what makes the mutual and reciprocal recognition of it in another soul so magical.

Why them and not another?

We love and lust after the ones who aren't good to us or who are no longer interested in us.

We don't notice or are not attracted to the ones who would be good for us.

We fall out of love with someone, wishing we hadn't, because it would have been so much simpler if we could have just stayed in love.

We fall in love with someone when we don't intend to and struggle to remove their touch, their gaze and the way they made us feel from our minds.

There are many things we can make happen in life on our own timelines and through our own willpower. Love and its appearance or disappearance into our life is not one of them.

Yes, there is nothing rational about love at all.

This book will give you the knowledge to understand the love journey after divorce and why it's such a different journey to the one we walked in our twenties and thirties to be married. It is, like my first book, *Seconds Please: Lessons on life, love and self after divorce,* the book I wish I'd been given to read before I jumped back into the dating pool after my own divorce.

Naïve. Seeking someone to love me. To make it all better.

I left my marriage clueless to the soul journey that was ahead of me. In fact, the word 'soul' was not even in my vocabulary. That word belonged to the 'woo woo', the spiritual and the hippie people of the world. And I was not one of them. My mind was focused firmly on finding my next someone.

Being single for me at that time was just not a desirable option, and I thought it meant something negative about me if I didn't have a someone on my phone or in my bed loving me.

How much a woman can change.

Whatever your beliefs in love that you may hold right now—completely jaded about love and reading this book only because it's been gifted to you, scared to open yourself up to love again because of the hurt and disappointment love has brought to you in the past, or fully open, ready and on the spiritual love path, there is something invaluable I want you to know.

Everyone deserves to be loved, appreciated and seen for all they are, even if they've never experienced that kind of love and appreciation before.

Everyone is capable of attracting and enjoying a love like this even if they don't know how in this moment. Everyone is worthy of experiencing this. We must sit as conscious adults and admit this. Not that we are at fault or that there is something innately wrong with us or we are lacking. Not that we are a failure to have divorced. Only that we showed up to love as best as we knew how in the past. This encompasses all that was modelled to us as children and as young adults courtesy of our parents: the emotional tone of their relationships, the intimacies, the passion, the communication styles or the complete lack of all of the above.

We brought it all into our marriage, not knowing that

we did.

When we leave a marriage, we are ultimately breaking free of our conditioning and fear. This changes an individual's psyche immeasurably. If you don't know what I mean by this sentence, in reading this book you soon will.

Divorce is you living authentic to yourself. It is you no longer living a lie or for anyone else before yourself. And if you are the one who chose to leave your marriage, it's you expanding into the awareness that you are not a selfish person for doing this.

Whether by your personal choice or by consequence, this speed hump in time is a part of your love journey. A love that was no longer true for you, aligned with you or meant for you, has come to an end in your life.

And while you might not see it in this light just yet, I'm so pleased that it has. Because the reality for most of us is that we weren't ready for 'the one' to have walked into our lives when we were younger and barely knew who we were or what really made us shine.

Every love, every lesson, every moment leads us to the one. And in that moment when they do show up it will all make sense to you. You will understand why they couldn't have showed up in your life any earlier than they did.

That, I know for sure. Whether you believe in the one or not.

Xo

However you arrive to this book

Maybe your marriage has only recently ended. Maybe you are preparing yourself for a possible divorce and everything that might lie ahead for you. Perhaps you've been separated and dating for quite some time.

However you arrive to this book, it is the right time. I believe in divine timing and meant to be. In the dance that is your soul path, your destiny and free will all combine into one—in synchronicities and coincidences.

I believe it is necessary for us to experience contrast in our life to grow, expand and appreciate life: negative experiences that enlighten us in such a way that they wake us up and lead us onto positive experiences.

We don't have to be spiritual or soulful to acknowledge that there is a lot to the energy of life that is magical, beautiful and beyond our full understanding and explanation. We don't have to be woo woo to admit that. And so, with this book, I'd like to invite you to let me combine both the rational and the spiritual journey of the love and soul into one. This is essential because if love was a rational emotion and journey that we could just switch on and off as we please, then you would still be married. No one takes a bomb to their life by asking for a divorce for rational reasons; you would just stay married if you were leading with your rational mind. It would almost always have been the easier option.

A divorce happens because the discontent and unhappiness of the soul can no longer be fully silenced by the voice of the rational, logical mind. It grew to a point of no longer being able to be ignored.

Soul misalignment.

Whether theirs or yours.

It reveals everything to us.

PART 1

Understanding Love, Marriage and Divorce

Where I present the case that you getting a divorce might be the best thing that could ever happen to you.

WHAT IS LOVE?

"Love is about being able to be with another person as they are, just for themselves; not because they meet our expectations, not because they are doing what we want, not because we find them physically attractive, not because they meet some ideal, not because they are behaving themselves, not because they make us feel good. We just 'meet' them as they are. To 'meet' someone means we see them for who they truly are, we accept them as they are and we engage with them as they are. We truly see them for themselves. Just sitting and being with someone and listening to them lets that person know that they are worthwhile and worthy just for being themselves. They know they don't have to do anything more than this in order to be lovable."
— Cynthia Hickman, The Eyes of Love:
Bringing Out the Best in Each Other

Above is one of the most beautiful statements I've read that encapsulates unconditional love for another. Most of us have sadly only experienced love and loved another with conditions.

If you do this or treat me like this, then you are loved.

If you look like this, you are loved.

If you make me feel a certain way about myself, you are loved.

If you hurt me, I will take my love away.

If you disappoint me, I will take my love away.

If you leave me, I will take my love away.

If you change and I don't agree with it, my love will change.

Love is vital for our wellbeing as humans. We need it to thrive and we seek it from the humans around us from the moment we are birthed and arrive into this world. Without love, we may have survived physically in this world, but we would have not survived well psychologically. Love is necessary for humans, and we first learn how we have to act to best receive it from our parents.

Unfortunately, for many of us, our childhood love has come with conditions attached. Even if this is just in our remembered perception of our childhood more than it was the reality. How well you succeeded in school or in sport, your appearance, how well behaved you were, your easy-going nature. All of these external aspects set a child up to believe that they are lovable because of their doing, not their being. It leaves a child with a role within the family that they then take with them into adulthood. The responsible child who looks after everyone who becomes in time the responsible adult. The over-achiever who continues to equate success with appreciation. The under-achiever who continues to receive love and attention in any way. The funny one. The easy-going one. This isn't to say that your parents didn't love you unconditionally. Of course they did. The closest to unconditional love that many of us will ever experience is the love we have for our children.

But in our psyche as children, as we learn how to best receive love, attention and praise, we also take on a belief about who we need to be and how we need to act to receive it. This is when we learn what love looks and feels like.

This is the emotional tone that is then set in our psyche as a blueprint for normalcy. For a well-cared for and nurtured child, with parents who are in love and intimate with one another, then that child might be left with an inner emotional tone of 10/10 that is normal to them, one that they go on to replicate into adulthood. For an under-nurtured child with abusive or emotionally absent parents who fought regularly, they might be left with an emotional tone of 1/10.

Both go into adulthood replicating this emotional tone of love over and over again in their intimate relationships without realising. This is emulated in their choice of partners and relationships that they choose to stay in and settle for.

Have you seen yourself and your childhood in the above yet?

As adults, how does this look as we layer all of our love experiences upon love experiences in our psyche? The love we have received from our parents, the love and the heartbreak we've experienced during the entirety of our adolescent and adult experience. We see adults with closed hearts to love—jaded, mistrusting, shut off and even a little repressed. We see adults with open hearts to love—trusting, comfortably vulnerable, intimate. And we see adults with hearts ajar to love—hesitant, slightly less trusting, cautious.

Yet, we must remember this. Whatever life and experience might have done to shape your view of love and yourself up to this point, whatever emotional tone your childhood might have left you with as a point of normalcy, we arrived into this world as babies with beautiful souls and open hearts. Souls that desired and needed love, attention, kisses and cuddles.

As adults today, we might wear tough or independent armour. However we might present ourselves to the world right now, this essence is still true for everyone underneath all the fancy clothes, the nice house, how you style your hair, the car you drive. A desire and need to love and be loved unconditionally for who we are is true for all of us underneath it all.

Love exists within us all and connects us all. If we could embody this without armour, then love would be easy and love would be everywhere. It is only our armour of humanness that has complicated it. Love is the vehicle for self-growth. It gifts us feelings of connection, contribution, significance and even certainty, safety and security in the world.

It's why we attach and hold onto it when we find it. Why we protect and hold onto the relationships that give it to us so fiercely. And why it can be so hard to let go of even when we know the love is not right for us. Because in many ways, it is the cornerstone of our psyche for all of us. Whether we care to admit this or not.

WHAT IS MARRIAGE?

'If you don't know history, then you don't know anything.
You are a leaf that doesn't know it is part of a tree.'
— Michael Crichton

Marriage can be a beautiful institution for some.

In my work with individuals, I always freely share this. I am neither pro-marriage or anti-marriage. But I am pro-love and soul growth before I am pro-marriage. This view upsets a few. Normally the married ones. But it doesn't change the truth.

Love doesn't need marriage for it to exist.

Marriage is not evidence of love.

And many marriages that exist today are preventing some individuals from reaching their best potential and living at their fullest. Society has evolved and changed so much since the concept of marriage was first invented thousands of years ago. Marriage's actual primary purpose was to bind women to men, and thus guarantee that a man's children were truly his biological heirs. Through marriage, a woman became a man's property. This is the history of marriage. It was an institution we created for reasons of social order.

Can you see now why we find ourselves in the societal place that we are today with more marriages failing than ever? Marriage was about heirs and procreation, the alliances of families with one another, the passing down of any property and wealth to the next generation. It had nothing to do with love. Nothing to do with how well your partner treated or appreciated you, whether you had anything in common, or about sexual connection or attractiveness.

Yet, this is everything many of us desire from relationships today and leave a marriage seeking them from another partner. This is something for us to ponder now that we are living much longer lives than we did thousands of years ago when the social construct of marriage was invented. Most of us who are divorced or divorcing now would not be alive at this age if we had been alive in the past. Life was much more fleeting, many of us would have died by now from giving birth, from war, from an infection.

Yet, the institution of marriage still holds weight even though society has changed.

'To have and to hold, till death do us part.'

As I mentioned before, I am not anti-marriage or pro-marriage. I'm pro-love and being in a relationship that is healthy and loving for all individuals. But something for us to consider in the modern world is that what many of us desire from a partnership—love, connection, intimacy and understanding—is not what a marriage was actually designed for.

With so many of us now divorcing and viewing divorce as a personal failure, I want to ask, is there any truth in this? Is it really a reflection of you having not tried hard enough? In my professional experience, it is almost never this. No longer is the length of a marriage the badge of success or a reflection of a successful marriage. Society's view of marriage has changed entirely on this point compared to opinions of the past. And while the fear of change that a divorce might bring—financially, socially, emotionally—still exists, the desire for personal growth, happiness and what is ultimately soul evolution and soul expression is now greater than ever. Many people who have left marriages are leaving seeking a different depth of love, connection and relationship than they've experienced before.

Divorce for them is actually their consciousness evolving as a human. Not away from love but towards a more aligned version that is right for themselves. They are desiring it in a deeper, more soulful way than ever before— even if they don't know it yet.

THERE ARE NO WRONG PARTNERS
(Hence, We Should Have No Regrets Or Hold No Bitterness)

'You never meet the right people at the wrong time because the right people are timeless.'
— Heidi Priebe

I write this chapter knowing that it is easier to accept for those who chose or who are the ones choosing to end their marriages. A much more bitter pill to swallow for those who feel abandoned, mistreated or left behind.

However, the lesson remains the same.

There are no wrong partners. No wasted years.

They were precisely the being you needed for the stage of evolution that you were at when you met. Who you attracted and ended up marrying helped reveal to you your limiting beliefs which allowed you the opportunity to transcend them. This is as true for you as it was for your partner. Maybe you transcended your limiting beliefs or maybe they did. Typically, the one who transcended their limiting belief is the one who chose to end the relationship.

Almost everyone comes to their first marriage believing they needed it for reasons outside of themselves. This is typically a reflection of us having chosen a partner and having entered a relationship at an age where we barely knew ourselves and hardly understood our future needs and potential.

The clichéd stereotypes that I see so often here will ring true for many.

Men who thought it was time for them to settle down and be responsible. They'd been single long enough, played the field for long enough so they chose to marry the woman who ticked all the boxes. Or she fell pregnant to him, so they married, which was the responsible, right thing. Only to find themselves emotionally and sexually disconnected and somewhat bored many years later because he made the stability, security, sensible, right choice. These men typically end up with everything that was once their version of success on paper—the house, the family, the career, the money—but it lacks what their soul really desires: passion and a deep, loving connection.

Women who chose their partners because they were confident with money, successful and good providers. Men who had drive and direction and knew where they were going in life which ultimately saved her from having to step into these qualities for herself. She goes on to leave her husband because in time she begins to feel too controlled, repressed, manipulated and unappreciated. He is structured and controlling, and now she seeks freedom and wants to grow. After years of accepting less than loving behaviour from her partner and staying because she was fearful about providing for herself financially, she eventually reaches a point of 'I can't do this anymore, I'm done.'

Clichés. But true.

Relationships are often chosen because of a void within us. For example, a person will 'give me this' that I don't have in myself or 'they will save me from this'. This is an attempt to skip the necessary self-growth that eventually catches up with us later in life. The ending of love and relationships can take on a completely new level if we view them from this perspective. However, the lesson can be still hard to accept.

A soul entered your life at one point of your evolution where you were perhaps out of balance within yourself, until yours or their evolution outgrew the necessity for the other in the relationship. If someone left you, however they chose to do it, it's because their soul outgrew you and your dynamic as a couple. If you left someone, it's because your soul outgrew them and your dynamics as a couple. This is a bitter pill to swallow for some—that your time with someone ended if you weren't ready for it to end or didn't feel the same way.

Will we reach a point of soul evolution where we will not outgrow another? Yes, I believe that we do.

More about that later.

WHY ARE SO MANY PEOPLE JADED ABOUT LOVE AND MARRIAGE?

'The universe is going to give you the exact same lesson in different versions over again until you master it. This is one of the most single important laws you can learn about the nature of reality. Everything else builds upon this.'
— Maryam Hasnaa

How many marriages or relationships that exist in your social or familial world around you would you want to have for yourself?

Think on this for a moment.

Whose marriage would you want for yourself?

When I ask my clients this, I always hear a shade of the same answer.

'Only a few.'

'One or two.'

If we sit with this mind-blowingly low result, what is it telling us?

Not that love doesn't exist or that marriages are hard work that require large amounts of self-sacrifice and compromise; it's a reflection of couples staying in relationships and marriages where they are no longer in love or feel happy—or that they've outgrown—but family, obligation and marriage have kept them tied and together.

It's a reflection that so many love relationships today are going around in a never-ending cycle of repeated patterns and behaviours, compounded over time by many years of biting tongues, keeping the peace and the occasional argument when it all gets too much. A cycle that has repeated itself enough over time to slowly kill the emotional connection, deep intimacy and love.

It's also a reflection of how well so many of us see through the personalities and intricacies that others think they're presenting so well to the world.

And we wonder why so many of us as adults are jaded about love and marriage?! The result is couples and individuals who have not let go of relationships that they probably should have released years ago.

Look at what surrounds us. Look what we are modelling to our next generation. Consider what was modelled to us.

There is so little representation of what a truly loving, healthy, happy relationship looks like in most of our worlds. Instead, we are surrounded by a lot of settling, mediocrity, holding on and varying degrees of self-abandonment and tolerating in the name of marriage.

This is not where I want to hear you say, 'It's easier if I just stay single, then.'

This is where I want you to start waking up to the realisation that you having left your marriage means that you now get to be in and create the example for your children and for others that you didn't have represented to yourself.

There is no reason why you can't be in and find yourself in a relationship like the one or two that came to mind at the start of this chapter. No reason at all other than you just haven't been in it yet.

Some people meet their one that they connect with emotionally, sexually and intimately in a deep way early in life. They grow together and their relationship deepens in all the ways as they deepen as a couple. To meet this person early in life is like winning the jackpot. It doesn't happen for all of us. The truth is that most of us weren't of the energetic match capable of being in such a relationship so early in life.

This is why many of us meet this person later in life. We weren't ready for them to be in our lives any earlier. We wouldn't have known what to do with such a love and we certainly wouldn't have appreciated it.

It's why we will often marry and procreate with one person early in life when we are at the 'prime' age to do so but go on to meet our 'forever' one in someone else later in life.

We have, through life and experience, evolved enough in our souls to be ready and prepared for such a love. I wish more married couples who are dissatisfied and sticking it out realised this. Sometimes the most powerful and conscious thing we can do is to let go of a love that at one time was a match for our evolution but now is not.

When I was considering leaving my marriage at the age of thirty-four, I remember saying to a close friend, 'I feel like I'm in a marriage that my twenty-one-year-old-self chose for me. Only I'm not twenty-one anymore, I've changed, and this marriage hasn't really changed at all.'

Many of you reading this will resonate with that sentiment. It might just be slower or harder for you to accept if you are the one who has been left and are feeling abandoned or hurt as a result. To accept that your ex-partner saw this writing on the wall before you did, or at least wanted to do something to resolve it before you did or saw the need.

TO LEAVE A MARRIAGE IS TO BREAK THROUGH OUR CONDITIONING AND FEAR

Leaving a marriage is us breaking through our human conditioning and fear. Someone leaving us forces us to breakthrough both by consequence not by choice.

The marriage we chose for ourselves when we were in our twenties and thirties is the one that our family and social circle conditioned us to choose.

This is called human conditioning.

This relationship is typically a soulmate relationship. One which many outgrow as a result.

What I am starting to say more and more to my clients is this.

Actually, most couples who remain in this relationship for life are actually cramping their soul growth. Most will not be able to reach their fullest potential in this relationship.

Just like you would hinder your growth if you chose a career or job in your twenties with one company before you even knew yourself and stayed there for the rest of your life.

A common misconception of soulmates is that they are our 'one'.

Usually, they are not.

Our chosen marriage here is often: Someone of the same socioeconomic group. The same genetic level of attractiveness. Often from the same geographic location.

We chose this marriage sub-consciously. Our conditioning sees love and a great match in this union. This union leads us to see that it's time to settle down (whether you fell accidentally pregnant or not). Ignoring all the little red flags along the way because this union makes sense.

On a soul level many of us outgrow this connection as we grow and evolve into ourselves with age.

Whether someone chooses to stay out of a sense of responsibility to family and to children, to keep finances together, is someone's soul choice.

Grow and evolve as a new version of self. Or choose to remain married and, by consequence, remain more than likely a shade of the same person.

By choice or consequence.

The soul journey of love after divorce.

WHAT HAPPILY MARRIED COUPLES TELL ME

'Who you choose to be in a relationship with is one of the most important decisions of your life.'
— Jillian Turecki

I've had many professional success stories of clients who have gone on to find the most amazing partners for themselves after divorce. In my own life, I've also had some beautiful examples of couples who were still genuinely happy after many years of marriage to watch and reflect on. It might surprise you to hear what they think and have told me.

They look at unhappy, disconnected, grown apart couples and they wonder how they're still doing it to themselves—and why.

I also hear this same sentiment from many clients of mine who are divorced when they look at these married couples. Why are they still there doing that to themselves? I could never go back to that.

Once a person feels happiness, joy and a sense of freedom and appreciation to be all of themselves in life without criticism or constraint. Once they taste how that feels and they are loved for it, that becomes their new normal. They don't want to lose that feeling. Anything less than becomes a case of 'why would you do that to yourself?'

Sometimes we don't realise what we were settling for and tolerating to keep a relationship together until we are out of it. Time is always the biggest indicator of relationship dynamics that we came to accept as normal, only to realise after we leave and as we move onto our next love that they weren't necessarily healthy dynamics at all; it was simply all that we'd ever really known.

WHAT I THINK ABOUT MANY MARRIAGES

'Half of all marriages end in divorce—and then there are the really unhappy ones.'
— Joan Rivers

Unhappy, disconnected or unsatisfying marriages inhibit the evolution of a soul. So do relationships that we've outgrown but are staying in for reasons like children, finances or convenience. I'm not talking about the dynamic of the family unit here. Family and marriage are separate entities. I'm talking about the dynamic of two individuals within a couple.

You wouldn't believe the things that I hear. The things that individuals have tolerated, turned a blind eye to, settled for or believed about themselves to keep their marriage going and together—the absolute rubbish that some people have put up with in the name of marriage and staying married.

And people still feel guilty and a sense of failure for wanting to leave or a deep sadness for someone having left them after treating them miserably for years.

Affairs and cheating. Sometimes repeatedly over years.

Emotional abuse and manipulation.

Financial and emotional control.

Purposefully belittling their partners.

Lying.

Horrible, repeated name calling and mind games.

Gaslighting.

The slow slippery slope where we bite our tongues and keep the peace over little things in the early stages of our marriages that are 'not a big deal'. Only to find ourselves keeping the peace over things much larger many years down the path. Behaviour that at the beginning we would have never tolerated or accepted. Behaviour we would never have imagined we would end up having to tolerate in time.

This, all in the name of marriage and keeping a marriage together.

This slow, slippery slope.

I understand it, I truly do. It was my own personal journey over many years that, over time, cost me my confidence, self-worth and self-esteem. A path that took many years to rebuild because so much of what I was tolerating crept into my psyche over the years.

It was one of the most humbling things I had to accept after my marriage ended. Just how negative staying in my marriage had been for me over the cumulative years I was in it. Even though I thought I'd done a strong and wonderful job of not letting some of the negative dynamics affect my sense of self, over time they had.

I am not anti-marriage or pro-marriage. I am pro adults being in loving relationships with partners who love and accept them beautifully for all of who they are. Moreso, I am pro individuals being in relationships that bring out and celebrate the best in them.

For me, the question is never about marriage and whether it is a good or bad institution.

It is about love and the quality of love that exists between the couple.

Seeing through the façade of 'successful' lives and social constructs like marriage is my profession. In my profession I am allowed to glimpse behind the façade of both through talking with my clients in our private sessions. They can share with me—without restrictions—what's really going on in their minds, their relationships and what's not going on in their bedrooms.

I've heard it all. And I hear it all without judgement.

Many of my clients are the 'villains' for ending their marriages in the way they have or they are the victims of someone having ended their marriage cruelly.

Working in this space has changed my values and perceptions entirely about humans and what we strive for and value.

I no longer desire the things I used to desire because I see and hear how unhappy, trapped and miserable so many people truly are with all those 'values' that many of us once bought into and deemed as success.

It's lost all of its gloss to me as I'm sure it has for some of you here.

The beautiful home. Happy family life. The obligation to keep it all together because they've worked so hard for it and sacrificed so much—because they're viewed in such a way for having what they have. The institution of marriage is heralded as this wonderful thing that we must perpetuate to uphold the values of society.

The values become the trap.

That's not love. That's marriage.

We weren't born on this earth to one day get married and forever stay married—happily or not.

We were born to love, to expand and to grow as a soul and enjoy a life experience defined by love.

My soul would choose love and that experience over marriage any day. Even if that means having to leave a marriage to be able to find that love and experience again with another.

And actually, I choose it for you too because I know everything that it will lead you to in time.

Even if you don't feel this way in this moment.

A more expansive life.
A more expansive soul.
A more expansive love.

WHY ARE WE SEEING MORE DIVORCES NOW THAN EVER?

'I do not believe that there were more happy marriages before divorce became socially acceptable, that people tried harder and got through their tough patches. I believe that more people suffered in silence and abandoned their true feelings.'
— Ann Patchett

There is a lot of discussion around the throwaway culture many perceive exists around relationships and marriages that end today, as though people are no longer trying as hard as they did in previous generations (or as much as they should). There is talk that we, as a society, no longer value family and commitment like we once did.

My professional experience is that for the majority of individuals, this is an unfair narrative. Very few leave a marriage without deliberating over their decision and the consequences for everyone involved for a considerable period of time first. This is often an internal process— sometimes for years—before it is expressed outwardly.

What might seem like an out-of-the-blue decision was often far from sudden in someone's head.

In fact, statistically, we know that many individuals stay

in a marriage for twelve to eighteen months longer than they perhaps should have and for every reason that they're later criticised and accused of not caring about—family, the children, everything they've built together.

Before they leave, these individuals sit with a lot of turmoil, self-doubt, guilt, shame and fear for wanting to leave or for having left. Even more so how their loved ones will react and deal with a separation.

I meet very few individuals who have not deliberated silently to themselves for a lengthy period of time about what to do, often for years before they ever discussed with their partners about their intention to separate or that they felt the relationship was over which tends to sadly come as a complete surprise to them.

So why are people leaving marriages and asking for a divorce more now than ever before? Simply put, because they can. In previous generations they either couldn't or at least felt they couldn't. Trying to compare divorce statistics now with those from previous generations is like trying to compare apples and oranges: two different periods of time with two different kinds of societal structures existing around them.

This is why we are currently seeing an increase in divorces particularly in the Generation X (individuals born mid-60s to 80s) and Baby Boomers (individuals born between 1946 to 1964).

In my opinion, it is a flushing of the pond of relationships that perhaps should have ended earlier but didn't because society frowned upon it more then.

These marriages consist of individuals who had outgrown their partners in many ways but who stayed for reasons like family, fear, finances or responsibility.

This also looks like individuals who came from parents who had divorced or who had unhappy marriages. They desired to create a home life and relationship for themselves and their children that was the complete antithesis of their parent's relationship and childhood experience. However, they then find themselves having created a wonderful family unit but alongside an empty, disconnected and sometimes unsatisfying relationship.

While it might be true that they passed down to their children an improved childhood experience, that over emphasis on family and children didn't facilitate the loving relationship that they necessarily imagined for themselves.

Divorce just wasn't seen as an option in the past like it is today. It wasn't as socially accepted and therefore happened rarely. Someone really had to be suffering terribly within their marriage for it to be socially justifiable to leave— domestic violence, persistent adultery, and behaviours sadly associated with addictions.

But even then, many women and men often stayed in these marriages because of the stigma of divorce but also the lack of support and financial capability to do so.

Therefore, the narrative had to become that family comes first, family is everything and staying together for the children is the responsible and best parenting choice.

Individuals, especially women, had no real choice to model anything else differently even if they desired too. Staying married and keeping the family together became the sole focus and the suburban dream and version of success.

It was the belief that being in a marriage, for better, for

mediocre, or for worse was what we should first aspire to. And everything in life outside of that was to be built up around it.

This works perfectly of course if the marriage is built on a strong foundation of love, connection and intimacy that continues to exist throughout the marriage. It works less perfectly if that foundation changes or gains many cracks over time to the point of barely being held together.

Like a house of cards, marriages like that will always, in time, fall down. Now and in future generations.

In many ways it is a different level of human consciousness and awareness today than was lived in previous generations. The husband went to work all day. He earnt the money and provided for the family. That was his job done. He came home to a cooked dinner. Spent some time with the family, if at all. His emotional contribution was often very little. The wife's role was to stay home and care for the children. Her emotional contribution was everything to the family unit. All of this with the occasional holiday thrown in.

It was the accepted system and social matrix of behaviour that many of our parents followed and, as a result, many of us also followed without much thought given. First, we do this, and then we do that, and then this, and then win—we are successfully adulting.

Personal happiness, personal growth or personal fulfillment really didn't form a central point of anyone's thoughts or conversation. Back then, society really didn't support personal growth or soul evolvement. It supported a man to work from nine to five in the same job for thirty years and for the woman to stay home and be the housewife.

That was the narrative and accepted social structure that men and women lived in.

Quality of life is determined not just by our financial status and lifestyle anymore. As adults now, personal growth, happiness and soul evolvement are what many of us prioritise and desire. Even if they don't use those words and recognise that this is what they're really seeking—for a life and love that feels as good on the inside as it looks on the outside. One that is true, authentic and aligned with who we are.

The manner in which the level of human consciousness has now grown and evolved is because it has the capacity to do so.

I write the above paragraphs knowing that some will have read this and see their own relationship or marriage in my words and have realised much about themselves.

Men of previous generations may have desired to leave but they didn't because to do so was to abandon a dependant wife with little financial earning capacity of her own and children who relied on him too. There was too much shame, guilt and shirking of responsibility required to walk away, so they didn't. Personal desires and needs were sacrificed, and any feelings of dissatisfaction were put to the side for the greater good of everyone involved because of responsibilities and a 'family first' mentality. This man instead threw himself into work, sporting pursuits, the pub and anything that gave him more freedom out of the home as the coping mechanism.

Women of previous generations couldn't leave a marriage because they were so dependent on their husbands and the family unit for financial survival, for social standing.

For security, stability and safety. We have to remember that up until and throughout the 1970s, The Marriage Bar required women to give up their jobs once they were married and women were not allowed to get a mortgage without needing a male guarantor. In many ways, women did not have the same rights or opportunities as men.

This woman threw herself into her children and built a beautiful home. She lived and looked the part. She identified with this role. And she sat with her friends and they moaned and gossiped about their husbands to one another and what they were doing or not doing over cups of tea and coffee to socially connect. She hoped to not come out feeling like the worse off woman in the room which justified why she was staying in her own marriage but also gave her something to talk about with her husband 'can you believe so and so is doing this...'

It would be naïve of us to not consider that all of these social structures, restrictions and beliefs were not created purposefully to keep adults in social order and that the trauma and fear of restrictions and beliefs of previous generations haven't been handed down to both sexes as learnt behaviour.

All of this keeps men and women in a cycle of woundedness and co-dependency, unable to stand in their own power, their own brilliance and in their full confidence alongside and in love with another human being in their own power, brilliance and full confidence—all because social structures and conditioning didn't support or allow them to leave.

It is a very different energy. Two humans at their best. Equals. Choosing to be together. Not stuck with one another. In love. Choosing to be with one another.

A very different energy than is found in most marriages today. This is something I have no qualms in saying despite the controversy it might bring because of the number of conversations I have with so many individuals about what is really happening in their lives and marriages.

Women may fear the financial, familial and social consequences of change if they were to leave but they now have more opportunity than ever to be financially independent and strong and to carve their own lives without having a male partner at the centre. It is often the belief in their own capabilities that they lack and a lack of awareness and education to know what to do next now that they are making all the big life decisions on their own. Yet, if women look around today, they can see more and more women thriving in their lives post-divorce.

Men may worry about the financial consequences of change and the fallout it might cause in some of their relationships with friends and family if they were to leave, but they are growing more and more in their emotional awareness than previous generations. More present and involved fathers. Better connected socially with family and friends. And being that most men were typically the main provider for the family, their earning potential and ability to thrive financially into the future often remains unchanged. It is often the fear that their role as a father in the eyes of their children may diminish or change if the marriage was to end. That their standing within the family may be tarnished. Yet, if men look around now, they can see more and more men thriving in this space post-divorce and with their relationships with their children still intact, loving and connected.

Yes, divorce is only happening now more than ever because it can. Not because we care less about love or relationships or need them any less. Not because we don't value marriage but because we desire to be married to someone that genuinely loves and cares for us on an intimate level.

All certainty that someone must stay with you forever has been removed from marriage now. There are no guarantees. An individual has to want to and desire to stay with an individual. No one is beholden to another.

Many are not happy to see this forever safety, security and certainty around marriage start to slacken and disappear. I hear from these individuals in my emails and my social media DMs, many disgusted with the work that I do in this space and the way I support people to leave unhappy marriages.

I am, they say, encouraging divorce.

The truth these individuals in my inbox are ignoring on a soul level. There is no certainty in love and no guarantee that someone will continue to love you and feel the same way for you. And there never has been.

There was only ever certainty in marriage and marriage is a social construct we created as humans. Marriage for those who feel disconnected, dissatisfied, abused, taken for granted, or who have grown out of love with their partner is not a wonderous construct. It is a trap. One they wish they could slide out of.

And someone who is staying in a marriage because it feels right or responsible. Or because they want to keep their financial assets, home and lifestyle together is not contributing to the growth and evolvement of our society. They are actually contributing to the social order that marriage creates. The social order that is keeping them trapped.

No wonder the journey to finding love after divorce is such a different one.

We are moving against the social order that many around us are still in happily or not for either reasons of love or safety/security.

We so often have to upset and disappoint so many that we love on the pathway to choosing ourselves, our happiness and having the courage to voice it.

Love after divorce is a different kind of love entirely. And it will require a more evolved, better version of self if we hope to do it successfully. Otherwise, we will only go on to repeat our past patterns and conditioning.

I WANT YOU TO START SEEING THIS PERSPECTIVE
(if you don't already)

My desire is to bring everyone closer to love with a kindred spirit, recognising that for some this means having to first leave something they've outgrown. Often that thing being a marriage.

I'd love for you to sit with this.

Imagine what kind of world we would be living in if the majority of adults, instead of the minority, were in a relationship that was loving, passionate, connected, healthy, fulfilling—one that celebrated the best in both people. Beautifully loved up couples everywhere. Living life as their best selves.

Imagine the flow-on effect into the world of witnessing this kind of love and its impact on our children who live and learn vicariously through us.

I want you to start seeing the limitedness, inertia and heaviness associated with so many marriages around you—if you don't already. Not because marriage is an outdated or negative institution, but because there are too many couples still married when they perhaps shouldn't be. Envisage what this is contributing to our society, our children, our values and our collective evolution.

I want you to begin imagining this.

Imagine if the majority of adults had a full emotional and energetic scope to completely focus on all of the outside elements of their life and self because the love relationship of their life was easeful, balanced, caring, loving and allowed them the energetic space to do so.

There was no drama or unfulfilling relationship dynamic worrying them or clouding their thoughts, essentially sapping their energy on a daily basis. No home scenario or relationship they had to manage. Nobody ghosting them, lying to them, manipulating them. No disconnection emotionally or physically. No negative emotions or thoughts they had to manage or rise above regarding their relationship situation.

Imagine what each individual could potentially create in their own life if they were free from the weight of all of this.

Society would be of a very different energy.

Adults awake and awakening into the fullest expressions of themselves. Thriving and loved up. Creative even. And free to be so.

Begin to imagine that.

WHAT DOES IT REALLY MEAN WHEN WE LEAVE A MARRIAGE?

'We have been socialised to think that ending a relationship means we are a failure. And yet, a relationship that ends can often be evidence of empowerment. It can be the moment we've finally said "enough" and chosen ourselves, perhaps for the first time. The reason relationship endings are such potent vehicles for expansion is that the death of the relationship is also the death of the people pleaser. It's the death of conformity. The death of tolerating mediocrity. Whenever a relationship ends liberation can begin.'
— Mark Groves

Leaving a marriage is us breaking through our conditioning and our fears. Someone leaving us forces us to breakthrough by consequence not by choice.

The marriage we chose for ourselves when we were in our twenties and thirties is the one that family and social circles shaped us to choose. This is called conditioning.

This relationship is typically a soulmate relationship. One that many outgrow as a result.

What I am starting to say more often to my clients is this: most couples who remain only in this relationship for life are potentially, more than likely, hindering their soul growth.

A common misconception of soulmates that we will explore later in this book is that they are our 'one'.

Usually, they are not.

It's why our own divorce can not only trigger us to feel fear and uncertainty but also trigger those around us too. Our behaviour is going against the expected norm and social order. We are choosing different for ourselves. And we are no longer choosing to tolerate what many around us are still choosing to tolerate and buy into.

Not everyone is comfortable with having their perceptions of relationships threatened.

It's why many people can feel selfish, guilt or shame for wanting to end a marriage. It's why those who have been left can feel abandoned and more alone than ever before. The loss of the safety blanket of having a someone or being a someone for another, whether they treat us well or not, can be painful. We are very much breaking away from the pack and choosing ourselves when we leave a marriage. Sometimes for the very first time. It's why people-pleasing behaviour can be so often associated with marriages. When we are a people-pleaser, we look to put others' needs first before our own, even at the expense of our health, wellbeing or sense of self. Others' needs and feelings first. Ours second. Abandoning our needs like this is often linked to our self-worth and our fear of losing love and our place within the tribe of family.

People-pleasing is entrenched in a desire to belong at

whatever personal cost. We bite our tongues. Choose to not see what is really happening in front of us. We keep the peace at the abandonment and detriment of ourselves until the personal cost becomes too much to bear—too hard to ignore or distract ourselves from. Or our more grown-up children look to us one day and let us know that they 'can see you are not happy why are you still there?', giving us permission to leave. Removing the risk and fear we'd been carrying of leaving a marriage that might potentially have cost us a relationship with our children.

When someone leaves a marriage, it is because either the dissatisfaction and consequences of continuing to stay in the marriage wakes them up. Or the arrival of someone else into their life and heart has woken them up to what they now need in a lover and partner.

In life, humans, big and small, are either moving forward and making decisions to avoid pain or they are moving forward and making decisions towards pleasure.

What many don't realise is that it's not our humanness that chooses to leave a marriage. It is actually our soul underneath that is calling out for more, for better, for freedom. It is their soul's discontent with the way their human world is around them and how it's making them feel.

When we leave a marriage, we are choosing to listen to and move forward with our soul over the voice of our mind though often not even realising that we are.

'You have to decide with your heart and not your head. That's the only way you'll have peace with your decision.'
— Kate Rose

A marriage ending is a soul wake-up call.

Whether it was your choice or not. Someone had a wake-up moment. To everything they once believed and bought into. Everything they thought they once wanted. In whom they believed they were and who they thought they needed to be to receive love from those around them.

It's why the love journey after divorce is so different.

You are different by consequence from having left a marriage and from having to walk away from the conditioning that you once bought into and believed was the dream. This is the same dream that those are around you and still married are still buying into or at least pretending to behave like they do so they don't lose 'everything'.

A choice was made from the point of someone's soul when a marriage ended, that their personal happiness mattered more to them than everyone else's happiness, expectations or responsibilities placed upon them. They've made the choice that their personal happiness matters more than the money, the home they love or the lifestyle they enjoy. And the personal choice we make now once we leave a marriage is to either continue living from the point of our soul or to fall back into the trap of leading from our humanness—choosing what society deems is sensible for us, choosing from a place of ego or from how we like to be seen or viewed by others. Choosing from a place of wound or from a place of worth.

We either awaken further or we fall back to sleep.

A LOVE NOTE TO MEN AND WOMEN BEFORE WE GO ANY FURTHER TOGETHER

'Men marry women with the hope they will never change.
Women marry men with the hope they will change.
Invariably they are both disappointed.'
— Albert E. Einstein

I hear these two sentiments from men and women all the time.

Where are all the good men in the world? and;

Where are all the good women in the world?

Both sexes feeling and expressing the same things.

Let's talk about why both sexes feel jaded by the other.

It surprises many women to hear this, but many men do want to meet the right woman who adds to their life. To be happy, live in peace, enjoy the simple things and have amazing sex until the sun goes down.

They don't want to settle and take on what feels like 'drama' as much as women don't want to settle or take on drama.

And many men are not interested in having casual sex as much as some women think. For many men, it's lost its appeal because it attracts a certain type of woman which just brings drama, stress and a certain level of crazy into their lives (their words, don't shoot the messenger!). Many men consider relationships to be hard work so they don't enter them lightly.

Women, knowing that it is the men's turn next, I'd love

for you to please hold any inner rebukes you may have about men knowing it's important to equally hear from them too.

While yes, many men may be adept at dodging blame. Professionally, I'd love to share with you that, in my experience, many women are well-skilled at projecting onto others.

Women can be well-practised at shutting a man down and for making him feel bad for having said the wrong thing. Which is why men shy away from saying the truth and tell you what they think they need or want to hear—they don't want to hurt or disappoint you. They don't want to fight. In fact, many have no idea about what to do with your emotions, so they do their best to avoid them.

Not all women reading the above paragraph are going to agree with my sentiment. But it is what men tell me all the time. A man's perspective is different because it is allowed to be—they are wired in a completely different way to women.

And if I can ask one thing in the defence of men today, it is for women to stop assuming or seeing men as being less evolved or less emotionally in tune as women. This is an unfair narrative I see many women hold and it is not a true reflection of all men.

Men are entirely different creatures than women and many are trying more than you know. Many men are struggling emotionally more than they feel safe to communicate. All I ask is that we let them be who they are without criticism or looking down on them.

I am always going to be an advocate for having more strong men at their best and in their power in the world today as much as I am women. We need more of both than ever. I write this knowing that both sexes are unwittingly going to disappoint others and hurt others on the pathway to becoming this—their behaviour being the reason why you hold the view that you do.

What I hear from men:
- So many women are anxious and needy.
- It's so easy to manipulate women because they need attention and to be loved so much.
- Women expect us to look like something out of a magazine with a six-pack. She doesn't even have one.
- Everyone wants a guy who is financially secure or successful. I don't want a dependant or someone who needs saving.
- So many women out there are nutty.
- There is more peace in my life when I'm not in a relationship.
- I don't know if I want to be in a relationship again because I end up losing all of my freedoms and feel controlled.

Many women don't trust men and view them with quite a large degree of caution. They feel manipulated and misused. Taken for granted.

More and more women are choosing to be single and stay single because the hurt that men have caused them has been traumatic. They are tired of the dating cycle and going through so many lousy, disappointing, manipulative men. They are focusing on themselves. They are throwing themselves into their careers. They are opting out of casual dating and choosing to hold out until they meet a guy who knows how to love them right.

What I hear from women:
- Men don't know what they want.
- I don't want another man-child who needs saving.
- Men are more interested in how a woman looks and her youth than what is on the inside. I feel overlooked and like I don't matter anymore.
- I look around and regularly don't feel good enough.
- Men lie to get what they want and then they disappear.
- There are very few good men out there now.
- The quality of men has dropped in the world.
- Every time I date a man, I'm disappointed and left having to pull together the pieces of my soul. I just don't know if I can do that anymore.
- I'm happier on my own focusing on myself.
- It takes me a long time to trust a man now.

Actually, if you're in the pattern of attracting these types of men and women in your life and this is what you believe, then it says more about you than it does about the men and women in the world.

Men in their woundedness.

Women in their woundedness.

Projecting at one another what they fear and believe about love from the perspective of their past experiences.

Attracting and pursuing this same energy over and over again in others as a result because of their view of the world.

If we look below the surface of what I hear so often from men and women, what is it that we can see?

A burning desire for the same things.

Love.

To feel appreciated.

Freedom.

Not to cheat or be disloyal, but to just be themselves.

Understanding.

Safety.

Peace.

Security.

Room for growth.

I invite you to lose your judgement and criticism of the opposite sex and to instead see the similarities.

To stop needing the opposite sex to be different or better for you and to see the potential for good and amazing in them.

They just are what they are.

A soul desiring to be loved, to connect and to be valued like you. Just moving in a different way than you do.

Neither better or more evolved than the other.

Both evolving in their own way.

There are going to be some of the opposite sex who are going to be good for you. And there are going to be some who are not. There will be some who will bring out the best in you and some who will not.

This says nothing about the entire opposite sex.

It speaks only to the individual.

See the similarities.

PART 2

The Finding Love Journey After Divorce and Why It's Different

WHAT WE NEED TO UNDERSTAND ABOUT OURSELVES AS HUMANS

When the soul knows something is off in a relationship, nothing you do can make that feeling go away. It will disturb your gut, it will set up shop in your mind, it will put a tonne of weight on your heart. Until you stop ignoring it. Stop ignoring it.

What are we as humans?

When I ask this question, the response is almost always centred around our physical body and our physical representation as a human. And yes, we are that. Our physical human body is that of a Homosapien. We all have a body and a brain with a thinking capacity and the ability for speech that makes us entirely unique and consequently dominant in the animal kingdom world.

However, to look at a human with only its physical body as its representation is to dismiss the real essence of what makes us fully human.

It is to dismiss the magic.

The soul.

Quantum physics can now tell us when the soul and our consciousness, enters the human body at the moment of conception. We see it in the petri dish during the IVF process.

At the beautiful moment of conception there is a halo that can now be seen in the lab when the sperm enters the egg. At that moment, scientists know that the cell is viable, meaning it will grow into a foetus. The halo is indicative of the strength of the cell (the cell now called a zygote—the beginnings of cells becoming a human), and they use this indicator to choose the strongest one in the petri dish to transfer into the mother during the IVF process.

That halo moment has been identified as the moment the soul enters the zygote. It is the moment that the wonderful uniqueness that is you enters the beginnings of the growth of your physical body.

This is the point where science in many ways meets religion and spirituality—whatever your beliefs might be.

Your soul energy enters your physical body at conception.

You are made up of two separate parts.

You are the soul.

And you are the physical body.

Science can show us now that we are more than just our physical bodies. We are energy that is taken from the energy present around us at the point of our conception, which is then placed into a body of mass—the beginnings of our physical body.

A quantum biologist whose work I love, Dr Courtney Hunt, explains this beautifully, almost like our souls having made its way to the front of the queue at a deli counter. We're given a number, your number is eventually called, you approach the counter and into the world you enter to become Susan Smith, whose physical human body will look like this, whose parents are Bob and Jane.

The magic of human existence. To ask ourselves how destined were we to become what we one day grow up to become? How much of our soul journey was already mapped out for us before we entered our human physical form?

Why is any of this relevant to this book?

Because today we see so many humans mostly leading their lives from the point of their human physical body—achieving, thriving, doing what is right, responsible, financially smart.

While all along mostly or completely ignoring their soul—how they feel, their intuition, their emotional world, what they actually desire and are drawn to. Until it becomes a scream.

We see a big disconnect in many humans now where much of their life and decision making is made from a point of their brain and humanness. And very little, sometimes none, is made from the point of their soul.

Divorce for many adults is the pivot point where the soul became so unhappy and felt so out of alignment with the physical human world and relationships created around it that it could no longer be ignored or quietened.

For some it feels like the first major pivot point in their life. However, if most of us look back with eyes now wide open, we can see other moments in our younger years, before social constructs of marriage, finance and responsibility were built up around us so heavily, where we made life decisions from our point of soul desire and for no other reason than because we desired to.

The teen or twenty-year-old person who moves interstate or overseas to travel, to take a gap year or to follow love is a wonderful example here. A life decision to leave a marriage is made from a point of someone's soul. Whether someone chooses to continue to lead with their soul in life after divorce or to even awaken to their soul as a result of it… well that's another journey.

It's why some people go on to change quite deeply as a person after a marriage ends.

Their values change, what is important to them evolves, they begin to look at their patterns and heal their wounds, they begin the process of waking up to themselves and the beliefs that lead them to become who they are. For these individuals, life often completely changes after a divorce. Their ideal partner changes too.

It's also why some people don't change at all after a divorce. They have no desire to change. They go onto meet the same kinds of partners next with the same kinds of dynamics that allows them to stay the same kind of person.

Their soul never really awakened. Maybe it did for a moment, enough for them to recognise their dissatisfaction and misalignment with their human physical world, enough to propel them forward. Only for them to return back to leading with their humanness again.

Have you seen yourself or your ex-partner in this yet?

WHY FINDING LOVE AFTER DIVORCE IS A DIFFERENT KIND OF LOVE JOURNEY
(some might say harder)

'You're not lonely. I'm just taking you to the next level of your soul journey and some people can't go with you.'
— Source Unknown

We have an unfortunate growing culture that fosters and celebrates outward success, possessions and technology, while downplaying the needs and desires of our inner world.

We can see this in both the younger and older generations. But increasingly in the younger now with the oversaturation of social media in our lives. What someone is wearing, driving, where they live, what they own, how they look, where they are tagging themselves on social media. All these titbits give you a glimpse into where they are holidaying and eating out without telling you where they are. A glimpse of the label that they are wearing without telling you what they're wearing.

Can we collectively 'lol' at the human race and ourselves right now?

All of these facets just add to the human physical form which is ultimately, to me, the avatar we use to present to the world how we desire to be perceived by others.

Material comforts are great to a point of course. Yes, they are also sometimes necessary. But without a foundation of connection, love and inner satisfaction, life and its meaning can begin to feel quite lacking.

Disconnected. Fake. Still, it feels not enough.

We can see this demonstrated in couples who outwardly have it all—successful, security, the beautiful home, family and life but who are nevertheless dissatisfied and feel a sense of disconnect and emptiness with it all.

Often, it's not until we leave a marriage that we are able to step back and take a look at what had really played out within it. What you both really prioritised. What that says about you. What it says about them. What it says about you both as a couple.

Understanding where we went off our soul path and why. Working through the internal beliefs and conditioning we hold and breaking down the human barriers present within us. All of this is us taking down the shields that life has built up around our hearts and souls.

This is no snapping of the fingers, no overnight process.

This is an undoing process that occurs slowly over time. A gradual lowering of our protective shields, of our need to be seen and perceived in a certain way. A growing comfortableness to be seen for who we really are. A process that in time returns us back home to the beautiful loving soul we really are and always were before the world happened to us, back to the soul that we were when we took our first breath. Innocent, loving, carefree, trusting, adventurous, playful.

This process of undoing allowing us a greater capacity for both self-love and love for others. As uncomfortable as it often feels along the way.

This opens us up to new deeper, more meaningful connections with ourselves and with our next partners in the process.

This is why finding love after divorce is a different journey and process to the one that led you to find a partner to marry.

Everyone was leading more with their humanness and their physical body to procreate, settle down, succeed and thrive when they chose a partner to marry in their twenties and thirties.

Very few of us had the level of spiritual awareness at that age to choose and love from the point of soul.

We were more a product of our conditioning than we were a reflection of who we really were on the inside.

We can look at the adult modern dating world after divorce and see three types of people we will encounter in the dating process.

Some humans leading entirely from their point of physical body and ego, unaware of their soul, unaware that they're living from their human conditioning and fear.

Awakening humans of different, varying levels and degrees. Leading somewhat from their point of human body and ego but in increasing amounts leading also from their soul.

And awake humans, leading and living entirely from the point of their soul: their physical world and relationships built around them in such a way that it supports their soul and its growth.

A sliding scale of awakening humans, egos and souls bumping their hearts and bodies into one another. Sometimes for a long time, sometimes for a brief time. Some mindlessly. Chasing the next hot thing or catch. Some evolving upwards to love, learning lessons along the way through the contrast of negative and positive experiences.

Some of them doing this consciously.

Some of them asleep to it all.

Hurting others and themselves along the way.

A mixed bag.

None of this journey or level of awareness was needed for us to find a partner to marry.

But if we wish to create a different future than the past and the relationship we have left behind, then this is your journey now—to evolve up.

IS THE GRASS ACTUALLY GREENER?

Is the grass actually greener when you leave a marriage? Ask a married person and in their answer, you will hear their fears. Ask a divorced person and in their answer you will hear everything they've learnt.

If ever I am having a session with a client who is weighing up whether to leave their marriage or not, this statement is almost always asked.

Is the grass actually greener? Will I actually be better off? And my children too? Shouldn't I just be grateful with what I have? Will it even be worth it?

The answer is quite simply that it depends on what you want. It depends on what you currently have.

Do you want more of the same with your partner for

the rest of your life or do you not?

At some point in all of our relationships, we must accept that the people we are in a relationship with might change a little bit, but not that much.

They are who they are and you are innately who you are.

And while almost everyone goes on to mature and evolve into themselves as they age, very rarely does someone change personalities and their characteristics entirely.

They are who they are, and you are innately who you are, and together you bring out certain elements and different qualities in each other.

We all know through experience that there are some relationships in our life that bring out more of our better qualities without trying. These relationships feel easy and the connection just flows. And some relationships bring out more of our negative qualities without trying. These relationships can feel like harder, heavier work.

Something that many of us like to forget is that we get to choose our life experience and the relationships we keep in our lives.

In fact, our relationships form one of the biggest pieces in the jigsaw puzzle of our life experience.

Some of you haven't been growing in your life because your biggest roadblock was in the bed next to you every night. Or they still are!

You get to choose.

So yes, the grass can actually be greener. In fact, it almost always is.

I don't personally know of many, if any, divorced individuals—and I know a lot through my work—who regret their decision, wishing they could reverse their decision and go back.

'Is the grass actually greener' is a fear and question only asked by those still married and weighing up what to do. They look to their separated and divorced friends and, depending on their social circle and perception, will see what they want to see.

Women will see girlfriends who are still single and wading through the dating world and think 'not worth it' because she's alone. They do this while completely overlooking the fact that this woman might feel frustrated with not having found a great man yet, yes, but who is deeply loving her life, her freedom and wouldn't change a thing for the world in the meantime. She hasn't found him yet. It's not a forever situation. She would never choose to go back.

And men will see friends who lost at least half of their everything that they built up and created, out there and dating the hot new chick only for it to go pear-shaped quickly and so they think 'not worth it' also because he's now alone. They do this while completely overlooking the fact that this man might feel frustrated with not having found a woman yet, yes, but who is deeply loving his life, his freedom and wouldn't change a thing for the world in the meantime. He hasn't found her yet. It's not a forever situation.

Unhappy and dissatisfied married people like to forget that it's not a forever situation for their divorced friends. It's just a moment in time.

It's very hard to perceive how life could look while anyone is in something that they're tolerating and settling in because of future fears of 'what ifs' and 'what could go wrongs?'.

Recently, I was out socially with a girlfriend and she ran into a group of school mums that she hadn't seen since she'd left her husband. As we were sitting there one of the mums came up to her and after the initial chit-chat, she asked my girlfriend with a face full of empathy, 'How are you with everything? Have you been okay? You poor thing.'

My girlfriend replied that she was fantastic, feeling better than ever, had met a new partner and that everything was going great.

When this woman left and returned back to her table my girlfriend turned to me and said, 'That's so bizarre, she's in an unhappy marriage, they've been in separate bedrooms living separate lives for years and she's worried about me? I'm worried about her!'

It's all relative, isn't it? The pain and dissatisfaction we choose to live with, accept and accommodate as 'normal'.

I always like to put it this way to my clients.

If I project everyone forward, divorced and married, and imagine them all thirty or forty years into the future. Where is everyone?

I'm almost certain that those who are now divorced and looking for love will have found their someone to love. They will have found their way and love will have come around again for them in a new, more evolved and loving way, aligned more than ever with who they have grown into being.

And those who are married and who continue to stay married to the same person will with almost certainty still be experiencing their relationship with a similar tone and shade as they are living it today.

We know this to be likely true because they will be the same two people with the same similar and established patterns of behaviour with the same ways of bringing the good and the not-so-good qualities out in one another as they always have.

If I look to my girlfriend and her school mum friend, how might that look and transpire? Almost certainly the school mum friend will be in the same situation with her husband if not worse into the future. And my girlfriend? She will be happy and have continued moving on with her life and forming relationships and experiences that are an amazing fit for who she is now.

We get to choose our life experience.

We get to choose who we keep in it.

Particularly within that inner sanctum of people we hold close to us.

We really do.

THE DIFFERENCE BETWEEN LOVE AFTER DIVORCE AND LOVE WITHIN A MARRIAGE

'Falling in love, you remain a child; rising in love, you must mature. By and by love becomes not a relationship, it becomes a state of your being. Not that you are in love – now you are love.'
— Osho

The beautiful energy of the love that comes after a divorce is that it's a choice. A choice to be with someone because there is nowhere else you desire to be.

Someone is there because they fully desire to be with you. Not because they are tied to another and have to be.

There are very few marriages where both individuals, hand on heart, could say that.

Sadly, this is how marriages can so easily support toxic and negative behaviours. Cheating. Affairs. Emotional and physical abuse. Keeping someone stuck in a repeated cycle of it all.

Even for the person who has fallen out of love with their partner, where the above dynamics aren't present, the ties that bind within a marriage can still feel suffocating. They feel trapped to remain in the union even though their heart is no longer fully in it.

For the individual in a marriage like this, it can feel hard to leave.

Someone in a marriage can sadly have the potential to get away with so much if they exhibit this personality, particularly if they know the other individual will more than likely never leave them because they love the family unit, the lifestyle that has been established, the dream they still believe in or because they know their self-worth and confidence is low.

Marriage for an abuser or a selfish person is the perfect playing ground to get away with it all and to have their cake of safety and security too.

The dating world after divorce is often talked about with much negativity. Men treating women badly and vice versa. I can't deny that, in many ways, there is a shade of this: neither sex understanding or fully appreciating the other.

But are many marriages around you, and the behaviours persisting in them, all that much better in behaviour than what we see in single and dating people? Really?

Those who behave badly are deservedly dumped or they move on to a next relationship to play out again their old patterns and conditioning is the only difference in the dating pool.

Instead of taking out their lack of growth and self-awareness on one person, they're taking it out on many, leaving a trail of hurt broken hearts.

The only pathway to rise above this car crash?

To not participate in it.

To come to a relationship as a more self-aware, conscious version of yourself over being an asleep less aware version of yourself.

To date, be in love and be in a relationship from a place of soul not from your humanness.

LIFE PATHS AND SOUL JOURNEYS

'Life is like a game of cards. The hand you are dealt is determined; the way you play it is free will.'
— Jawaharlal Nehru

This is not the book to explore where does the soul come from or even what exists beyond the soul. I need you to only accept or be open to accepting that the soul exists as a separate entity within the human body.

You are your human body.

And you are your soul.

The human body exists as the vehicle for your soul.

Two separate parts.

Science is aware of this and is trying to capture and learn more about the soul's entry into the human body at a centre called the European Council for Nuclear Research (CERN) in Switzerland. CERN is the site of a large underground hadron collider. The world's largest and highest energy particle collider that lies in a tunnel 27 kilometres in circumference and is as deep as 175 metres beneath the France-Switzerland border. Inside the hadron collider protons and electrons are smashed together at the speed of light to create black holes into the universe, simulating the halo that occurs when the sperm and egg collide at conception—a process that also occurs at the speed of light.

This isn't the book to discuss the implications for humanity if scientists manage to capture on their computers and understand the process behind how the soul comes to enter the physical body. Conceptually, once captured and understood, the soul can be captured and steered into any form on purpose. Not just a human body.

Sci-fi coming to life.

There is a reason why they call this discovery 'The God Particle'.

So, let's just allow ourselves to sit with the unknown of this.

We know the soul exists.

We know it comes from the energy around us at the

point of conception but we're not sure where from precisely, though there are many theories.

At conception, the energy around us enters the mass of who we are as a newly forming physical body. At our death, the energy within us leaves the physical mass of our body and returns to the energy existing around us. Mass returning to energy. This is quantum physics.

What I do believe is this.

Every soul comes to this earth with a potential in front of them. In many ways pre-ordained and in many ways perhaps quite laid out for us.

If we come from the energy around us at the point of our entry into the physical human world, then there is space for the argument that astrology and a reading of the planets at your time of birth might warrant some investigation, even for the most sceptic. And that anything related to energy healing of our soul body might also hold some weight.

Despite my own belief in free will allowing me choice in life over my life being completely mapped out for me from birth as fate, perhaps despite your own, we have to also leave space for the beautiful magic of synchronicities, coincidences and divine timings.

Because for even the most rational, logical minded individual we must allow space for the magic of life seemingly always being able to take us to where we needed to be. Shaping us to become who we were meant to be.

And we have to do this because most of us have experienced cases of this. Those moments where everything came together for us at the right time, at the right place. Better than we could have ever orchestrated for ourselves.

There is something in all of that.

Why come to Earth as a soul then? Who knows. There are many theories on this also.

But what feels intuitively right for me is that souls come to Earth with a potential to reach. And that it is our free will as to how long it takes for us to arrive there, what detours we have along the way and ultimately whether we face the soul lessons and growth we need to master to reach our potential.

We are either in alignment with our soul potential and in the slipstream of everything coming to us that is destined for us and that we deserve as a consequence, or we are out of alignment with it.

In soul alignment, our life, relationships and careers feel easeful. It feels like we're in our zone and they leave us feeling happy and at peace from a deep place within. We are lit up doing what we love and by living our life.

Out of soul alignment is where everything feels like hard work, a burden, a chore, where nothing is really coming together for us.

We see this modelled in those individuals in life who sadly never meet their potential. The family member or friend who fell into drugs or alcohol and their potential and life was wasted as a result. Their addiction wasn't their soul potential or journey. That was their free will getting in the way of their potential. That was them ignoring the soul growth and lessons they needed to have to evolve forwards in life having overcome their addictions.

Am I explaining myself well to you?

I know you came here for love and to understand more about the process of finding love after divorce. Why it feels harder. Why some loves and relationships have affected you like they have. And here I am explaining to you the soul.

Why am I talking to you about this?

Because if you have been through a divorce and left a marriage it is because the relationship was no longer in alignment with your soul. Or if someone left you it was because you were no longer in alignment with their soul.

It is a soul journey and it's important we understand that.

Because everything that needed to be learnt or could be learnt in the relationship with one another was learnt, and someone evolved out as a result.

Finding 'the one' after divorce for you is going to need you to be living your life while being in the slipstream of your soul path, and in alignment with who you really are which can only ever take you to your fullest potential.

That is the path where you will find the one, yes. It's also the path of least resistance where everything will come to you in flow that will lead you to your greatest potential and the freedom of your soul expression.

You are destined to be who you are meant to be, meeting the soul who loves and celebrates you.

Love lit up.

Power couples that light the way for others as much as themselves.

Living their soul life paths.

After leaving a marriage, the journey for many is going to first require you to find and be in the slipstream of your soul path and to be in alignment with who you really are first—sometimes for the very first time as an adult now that everything that was not that has been released.

If you've left a marriage or found yourself contemplating leaving a marriage for many years without having left yet, then you will know that the thought and process of leaving feels daunting, overwhelming, stressful and brings up all of your self-doubts and fears.

This is why.

You are realigning back onto your soul-path.

You are changing lanes on the one you were previously on.

Or if someone left you.

They are forcing you to.

THERE ARE ATTRACTIVE PEOPLE EVERYWHERE BUT SOUL CONNECTIONS ARE RARE

Someone can be so attractive on the outside and yet barely leave a mark or a dent on your soul's life path. They become just another one. Soul connections don't do that. They leave an imprint that remains.

I walk through life and am regularly drawn to attractive people. Women who are stunning. The way they dress or look. The way they hold themselves. They catch my eye and I appreciate them. Compare myself even.

Men who are handsome and attractive. The tone of their voice. Their build. How they are living their life. They catch my eye and I appreciate them. I appreciate their human physical form and how they present themselves. But this doesn't always translate to me being drawn to them as a person as a soul.

When we recognise this as we become more self-aware and accepting during the finding love after divorce journey, we must accept this.

There is a large quantity of people out there. But the quality of soul that is going to resonate with your soul... that is much rarer. I'd love for you to be less bothered by this lack of quantity for you and to embrace more the rare magic of quality, deep soul connections.

Their rarity speaks to their precious nature. Soul connections that become love connections are rare. And this is actually perfect. They would not be magic if they weren't.

ONE LAST THING IN CASE YOU FEEL GUILT ABOUT DIVORCE AND ITS EFFECT ON YOUR CHILDREN

You can either model to your children true love or you can model to them your conditioning for them to replicate.

Before I continue, I want to share that I am very much pro-family and a mum to two daughters. I am also a child of divorced parents.

I deeply value the family unit.

My support of divorce and belief that for some

individuals leaving a marriage is the best, most freeing thing they could do for themselves is not because I am not pro-family.

What we must see and realise is that love and family can continue to exist without marriage. In some instances, once the love and the family has evolved, the children and adults can be and are better for it.

Through my many years of coaching clients through separations and my own, there a several consistent themes. If there was a dynamic of lack of love, lying, cheating, manipulation, avoidance, downplaying of your intuition and feelings to keep the peace, distrust, control, emotional abuse etc., in your marriage, then your children were picking up on this emotional tone, this dynamic and the communication patterns and behaviours that go along with it, without you realising that they were.

Often without them even realising, they were being affected and shaped by it, regardless of how good a job you felt you were doing at hiding it from them.

What are we really teaching our children when we stay in a marriage for them?

We are teaching and showing them how to repress their emotions to keep the peace.

We are modelling to them what love is not.

We are teaching and showing them that their needs are not important in a relationship.

We are shielding them from the emotional reality of life, that not all marriages and connections last forever—and that is okay. It's not a failure or a poor reflection on you.

We are showing our children what it looks like to self-abandon by living vicariously through them and for them instead of equally for ourselves and our partner.

We are teaching them to fear and resist change over modelling to them how to handle change with growth, grace and resilience.

In some families we are modelling to them that lifestyle, possessions, keeping money together and the social façade intact is more important than the real elements that should be present in a relationship.

We are, in essence, conditioning our children to buy into and believe in the social construct of marriage that has made us feel trapped, stuck, unappreciated. We are teaching them to choose relationships and stay married for all the wrong reasons.

I hear from many men and women the deep guilt and sadness they feel for their family unit breaking up and changing as well as their worries about the negative impact that this will have on their children's lives.

But I would like you to begin considering the opposite: the negative impact staying in your marriage would have had on them into the future.

I very much understand your feelings and fears around this. My own guilt and sadness, with a healthy dose of fear around what leaving my marriage would do to my children, was one of the main factors that made me hesitant to leave.

As a product of divorced parents, it was also a desire and dream that I'd held—to be able to provide my children with that ideal home and family unit that I didn't have.

We actually had a relatively happy family life in the years of my marriage. My children were young when we separated and to them, we always presented as happy, loving parents.

But it was all for them. And that wasn't healthy for them or anyone.

As responsible adults, we must honestly sit with ourselves and ask, 'What am I really modelling and teaching my children in this relationship?' and 'Would I want to see my own child in a marriage like this?'

When many couples do separate, often the children are either:

1. Not that surprised
   or;
2. they have to adjust to seeing their mum and dad in future relationships with a new partner and behaving like someone in love does—intimate, touching one another, private moments just about them, being close. This is often a side they haven't seen completely in their mum or dad before.

It is untrue to say that children from homes where parents are still married and together are better for it or more well-adjusted.

This is a rubbish, outdated narrative. It is not always true.

Many children are much better off emotionally in the long-term as a result of their parents separating. Yes, in those instances where parents were unhappily married and warring, but also in those marriages that were disconnected, loveless and too heavily focused on the children and their happiness.

We start to really live the example that we want for our

children after a divorce and what we know to be true for ourselves.

We stop trying to facilitate their soul life path to the abandonment of our own. And, most importantly, we are being authentic.

Something I can say hand on heart is that my daughters are better off now for witnessing the woman that I am today—a woman I could never have been in my marriage, in character, behaviour or mindset.

One of the most important character attributes we can model to our children is to live true to ourselves and as the best version of ourselves. And to love and be loved by another in the same way that we would love them to be.

PART 3

The Three Loves

This chapter will give you the knowledge you need to understand why certain people came into your life and why some had to leave.

MY OWN WAKING UP
TO LOVE JOURNEY
(how I came to write this book)

'The ego self says: I will go where I want to go and pursue what I think is best. The higher self says: Show me where I am called to go. I let go. Guide me, I am yours.'
— Helena Wilde

Once upon a time I was a stay-at-home mum happily emmeshed in the world of two beautiful daughters, noisy toys and 'what are we going to have for dinner?' thoughts and conversations.

That was my world. And I was oblivious to everything outside of it. It feels like a far-away world to the person that I am today.

I was married, in my mid to late thirties and I had been with my ex-husband since meeting him at twenty-one. I was a product of divorced parents and while I didn't view divorce negatively, for me it was never something I saw myself one day needing or wanting.

In fact, I never saw it happening for me at all.

My marriage was one that outwardly looked quite perfect. Certainly, one that ticked many life-success boxes.

My ex-husband was a great provider. I had left my job and had happily slipped into the role of stay-at-home mum after having our two daughters quite close together. We had the nice home in an inner-city suburb. Our own business. Investments. We had some money to travel. Our social media life looked great. We had everything going for us that my younger version of self would have equated to us having achieved success and 'the dream'.

My ex-husband was a soulmate connection for me. From the same geographic area and socio-demographic group. He was the man that my childhood and parents conditioned me to choose and believe was a smart and strong choice. And on many levels, he was.

Dissatisfaction and a feeling of 'I don't feel happy in myself and in this relationship' and a 'have I outgrown this relationship?' type of thinking didn't arrive overnight.

It was a series of little and big things over time that happened and continued to build up in my psyche until one day I took my wedding and engagement ring off to clean the house and found myself absolutely unable to put them back on when I'd finished.

I remember looking at them sitting on my chest of drawers, not wanting to put them back on and wondering… what does this mean? Knowing it was a sign—and not a good one. But still I was physically and emotionally unable and unwilling to do anything more about how I was beginning to feel.

The thought of putting them back onto my ring left me feeling suffocated and heavy. It felt like doing so was a lie. And I couldn't bring myself to do it.

So, I didn't.

Feelings were brewing.

Waking up to the reality of my marriage and the personal price I was paying to remain in it became something that was continually reflected back to me. And however much I tried to join the dots of 'I should be happy and grateful' and 'we have a great family', however much I tried to keep the peace by managing my reactions and adjusting my expectations and needs, the waking up continued.

The differences between us grew more evident in my heart and eyes.

And they continued to until one day I sat and acknowledged to myself that if I was to run into my ex-husband today as a stranger, as the people that had become, not who we once were when I was twenty-one, that he wouldn't be my type at all. That I wouldn't be drawn to him in the room, even though I still loved him as a person today.

I did what most of us first do when we find ourselves unhappy in ourselves and in our relationships. I threw myself into distracting myself with other elements of my life. I joined the gym to feel more confident in myself again. I spent more time with my friends and connected back in with them. I started doing personal-development work on myself.

I followed the accidental cliché pathway that brought me to where I am today. I started studying to be a life coach. Started sharing motivational quotes all over my Instagram to my friends. My gym and working out pics. I became that person!

My journey to becoming a thought leader, coach and author on the topic of divorce and the emotional journey thereafter has been an accidental one. It was not at all on my list of life goals.

I mentioned it in my first book, and it is even more true now. If myself from 2015 was to knock on my door today she would not recognise who I am now. The depth of change in myself emotionally, energetically, even physically, has been that profound.

Despite all the personal work that I had done, it took me walking into a five-day personal development event to have the courage to ask for a divorce and to not feel guilty, wrong or selfish for doing so.

I arrived at the event thinking, *let's find out what is wrong with me and what I need to fix.* Instead, I was that woman who woke up to herself and the situation, realising that maybe it had not been all in her head or all her fault like she'd thought. I was the woman who came home from the event, sat her bags down at the front door and asked for a divorce before she'd barely sat down.

See. The cliché.

I say all of this with no malice or ill-will towards my ex-husband. It was a growing apart from our dynamic as a couple and of who I needed to be and remain being for our relationship to continue into the future that ended our marriage.

I felt so much guilt, fear and shame for wanting to leave my marriage that owning my decision and then having the courage to do something about it was difficult for me.

An intense period of five days of working on myself to understand my own limitations and low self-belief alongside finally being fully honest with a stranger in the room about the entire dynamics of my marriage and everything I'd been tolerating to hold it all together finally gave me the wake-up call I needed.

I left that event confident in my ability to create a different kind of future for myself as a woman. Confident of everything that was to come for me and with a solid sense of who I could become. And I left fully awake to what my life would look like in ten, twenty or thirty years' time if I didn't find the courage to do what I knew I needed to do by leaving my marriage that day.

I write this with full knowledge that my ex-husband would have an entirely different perspective on me and all of this than the one I've written above. As he's allowed to have this opinion.

Ultimately, I was the one who changed the rules on him. He hadn't really changed. I had. And so of course this made me all the things in his eyes: selfish and all over the place because everything that used to work on me no longer did and everything that used to make me happy and placate me no longer did either.

Even now we can still so easily slip into this same argument of all I am today that continues to upset his life order and psyche at times. Two very different people, now free to be who they fully are, who once were in love, who once needed the other to evolve through the world and to feel loved.

Funny how we change.

I could never go back to being who I was to remain married to him. I'm sure he would say the same.

It's a strange process this waking up to yourself and to a marriage that no longer fits.

You don't actually ask for it.

Eventually, you simply reach a point where you can no longer lie to yourself and it becomes harder to continue to even try to. It just continues to stare you back in the face.

How different you both are now.

How much happier, lighter and freer you feel when they're not around and in your space.

How much you seek out those moments of freedom away from them to almost survive the marriage.

I left my marriage in 2016 gung-ho and with one simple desire: to find the next someone to love me. The thought that it might take five or six years to find the right, long-term person never once occurred to me as a possibility.

Why would it have done?

I saw a psychic six months before I even left my marriage who told me that this was going to be my path. She saw that I was deliberating leaving my marriage. I'm not sure how good a psychic you needed to be to see that in me at that moment in time. Knowing what I do today after years of experience as a coach, I'm sure it would have been quite obvious. I hadn't been to a psychic for many years, and it was the roughest reading I'd ever had. She gave me a very forthright reading on how important it was for me to leave because of the dynamics that I was experiencing in my marriage.

In her words, 'If you don't leave now you will find yourself one of those women who come to me in their fifties wishing they'd left in their thirties.'

Say what you will about psychics, but she was on point. And I felt her reading in my bones.

But what she also told me was who I was going to become. I sat in front of her with a child in a pram, diminished, depleted, low in confidence, feeling so low in myself, dependant, and she told me, 'You can't see who you will become. But in five years you will be living in Sydney and flying back and forth between there and Perth where you daughters will still be and you will be comfortable with it all. It will take you five years to meet your person and he is living over there.'

When she told me I laughed. Other than you should leave your marriage, which I intuitively knew to be true, the rest seemed implausible. I wrote off much of the reading as BS as a result.

When I walked out of her room, I decided I was only going to believe what I wanted to believe. Some of it I could see was true. Some of it I didn't want to be. Some of it sounded ridiculous.

It wasn't going to take me five years to meet my person. As if. I'd never move away from my kids. I didn't like Sydney. What was she talking about? And yet five years later, here I am.

Doing just that.

Somewhere I once didn't want to be.

Her reading came true.

Despite me fighting it every part of the way.

Despite me not wanting it to be true.

After her reading my marriage continued to go gradually so far south that leaving was the only choice for my soul. I left my marriage six months later after giving it all I could continue to give.

I had two significant long-term relationships in the five years after my marriage ended: one that could have ended in marriage, but I said no, the other where I thought he was my forever, only for him to crush my heart by leaving me out of the blue.

I found myself at the five-year point after my divorce with every soul beacon in my life and career pointing me towards Sydney, feeling so truly comfortable in myself and my singleness that I'd even stopped looking for long-term love before leaving Perth. I knew love would show up at the right time, somewhere along the way.

I wasn't hiding from love. I was open and I was happily doing my own thing and thriving.

Life paths, destiny and that dance of free will and fate.

Free will and my ego weren't ready to let go of my marriage until it reached a terrible place for me. I fought it every step of the way. And my free will and ego insisted that it wouldn't take me so long to find my next partner. So, my every action and relationship choice aligned with this desire.

Yet my life path and destiny continued to happen anyway, neither gave a damn for my timelines, my hopes or my ego.

Fate and destiny man-handled me along my life path, gifting me the soul growth I needed to have, the lessons I needed to learn that, at times, I didn't want to have.

There is something to be said for being a strong, resilient and independent person like I am. Sometimes it takes more to crack us open and bring us to our knees. For life to break us. That was those five years for me. Strong, resilient and shouldering a lot. Until I couldn't anymore.

Through my own journey and through watching my client's journeys I've come to learn that for some, the love journey where we are truly ready for the one to enter, is a much different pathway than the one we imagined or hoped for ourselves.

It doesn't abide by our timelines or desires.

It doesn't care for our ego that we might feel doubt or worry that we'll end up alone.

It doesn't care at all.

It just does its thing. Nudging us and teaching us along the way until we reach a point within ourselves, not of being completely healed or awakened but one of actually being ready and genuinely open for love and everything life has to give us. This means being in soul alignment with who we really are and walking that path in readiness.

Because if I look back over the five years where I was trying to make love happen or wanted to make love happen, what do I see?

I see a woman who was more emotionally unavailable than she realised or cared to admit to herself. A woman who still had so much to heal. A woman who was far from who she was meant to be to meet the one and the man of her dreams. But who couldn't see it and didn't want to.

You can't become an author and coach on divorce and on the finding love after divorce journey without having lived the full experience first.

And I've lived the full experience.

Perhaps this was always my path?

Coming home to me had to come first before a love like I desired could show up for me. And that journey needed the contrast of losing myself and knowing what that felt like for it to happen.

I'd like to suggest that perhaps this might be true for you too. Even if you don't want it to be true. And what I'd love to share with you from the place of my own hindsight is to embrace it rather than fight it.

WHAT DOES A NEXT-LEVEL RELATIONSHIP LOOK LIKE?

'Your next relationship should take you to the next level of your life.'
— Jamie Rea

For many divorced people the path to finding love again starts with them first waking up to what love and a quality relationship really is.

All we know is what we have known. A sad truth for some of us to admit if all we have known is disappointment and a feeling of being let down, constrained or abandoned by love. I hear all the time. Relationships are hard work. They're not meant to be easy. Relationships take a lot of compromise.

But are they really? Because if someone says this to me then I automatically know that theirs is that to them. But does that mean that all relationships are characterised like this for others or should be?

Ah no. I don't think so.

This is simply a reflection of their personal experience of relationships.

The journey to finding love after divorce almost always starts here: a complete waking up to the dynamics of our past relationships and to what love and a quality next-level relationship actually is. A next-level relationship is not perfect. It is, however, easy by its nature. Not because one or both are biting their tongues or keeping the peace to make it so. Not because someone is over-compromising on their needs. Instead, it is complementary. It is easeful. It is characterised by evolving as a soul and shedding our negative patterns and behaviours, not circling around them again. And it celebrates both individuals for all of who they are—the light and the dark.

What are the qualities of a next-level relationship?
- The relationship is the easiest part of your life. Work can feel heavy, kids can be hard, but the relationship is the easeful energy in your life.
- Safe to express anything. No need to censor yourself or downplay what you need to express.
- Sex gets hotter. Deeper. More intimate. More exploratory even.
- Couples rarely, if ever, argue.
- No compromises. Certainly not on values and matters that are important to you because you are aligned.
- Communication gets better. When you are safe to express anything, you are free to communicate without hesitation. Therefore, it only continues to open up.
- Safe to grow and there are no limits placed on who you need to be for the love and relationship to continue.
- The relationship always feels safe. You know your person is never going anywhere. There is

no fear of their energy or presence leaking out to another. They don't desire to be anywhere else.

Often when we read through a list such as this it can lead us to ask, *does such a relationship like this even exist?*

I want to answer that yes, it does.

But this quality of a relationship is not possible with every soul that we meet. Not every soul will be a complement like this for us.

This soul will be unique.

And the wonderful essence about this discovery process? The soul that isn't for you will be the soul complement for someone else.

No soul is left unloved. If only we kept venturing forward with an open heart, willing to keep doing so, awake and leading from the point of their soul. Letting go of people in our life if we needed to until the right soul eventually found their place with you.

WHAT DO WE DESIRE FROM LOVE?

'What you'll find is that the only thing you really want from life is to feel enthusiasm, joy and love.'
— Michael A. Singer

There are the physical and character attributes that are important, unique deal breakers to you.

The one attribute we often forget?

Someone who will grow with me.

And if someone doesn't say this to me, I actually suggest it to them by asking—because this attribute is that important—*is someone who will grow with you important?*

The answer is always yes.

This almost always comes from a place of having outgrown someone in the past. They didn't do the 'work' or perhaps tried to but weren't able to maintain it long-term. Slipping back into their previous patterns that exist within their comfort zone after a time.

In the first five years post my divorce, I grew out of every long-term relationship that I had. We would start on the same page when we met, only to end up later, still in the same book, only now chapters behind to where I was.

If we acknowledge how hard it is to grow and change as individuals, then we have to accept how absolutely impossible, sometimes futile, a process it is to try and motivate or even carry someone over the line to grow and change.

Trying to help somebody who isn't ready or open is literally like trying to push porridge up a hill. Exhausting. Hard. Constant work.

Someone has to want to do it for themselves.

This pattern of growing out of different relationships in our lives is indicative of the soul's growth through love. It's where the love journey can start to feel hard or disappointing for some. And it's where I would love to introduce to you the three types of love that spiritually exist for all of us on our journeys.

Soulmates.

Karmic Loves.

Twin Flames (or 'the one').

You will out-grow a soulmate. You will also out-grow a karmic love. But you will not out-grow a twin flame connection. In this connection you will inspire positive growth in one another. This is the conscious desire of love: to be in union with one another and to continue to have the freedom to grow, love, express and evolve alongside one another while continuing to inspire and bring out the positive in one another.

Beautiful.

SOULMATE LOVE: THE PERSON FAMILY AND SOCIETY CONDITIONED US TO BRING HOME

The relationship you were conditioned to choose.
Not necessarily your forever person. In fact, most likely
someone you will one day grow out of or them you.

You will meet many soulmates in your life, and they will come in many different forms. Friends, lovers, family members. Souls you feel deeply connected with that are comfortable, safe, where you feel at home.

Your soulmate is actually not your 'one'.

This angers a lot of married people when I say this. It triggers all their fears around security, safety and certainty that they have placed around their marriage. It also knocks them off their pedestal of somehow being in a better life position than a divorced person.

But their anger or opinions don't make it any less true.

Your soulmate is actually not your one, as comfortable as they might feel to you.

In an intimate relationship, this is often the first major long-term relationship we experience. This is the fairytale of 'boy meets girl, marries and lives happily ever after' that we read about as children.

Before we really know ourselves, but while we are at the ripe age to reproduce, we unwittingly follow the expectations of what our families hope and expect for us, who society and our social circle expect us to end up with: our genetic and socio-economic equal. Even our own personal beliefs that it's time to settle down influence this choice in relationship.

It is love. It is a deep connection. But it is a love that we often outgrow because of the foundations listed above and the reasons why this love came together in the first place. Whether we choose to leave or stay is very much the personal soul journey and choice of both individuals in this relationship. One might recognise that they've outgrown the relationship while the other is happily comfortable in it.

From the outside looking in, regardless of how an individual might feel in it, this relationship simply looks right. It is the relationship that family and our social circle expected us to be in or hoped for us to have.

It feels safe. It brings comfort. It feels familiar. And it is usually supported by our social and family connections around us which keeps everything feeling bound together.

This can be a nice feeling for someone comfortably

married into this. A suffocating one for someone who no longer wants to be married into it.

The best analogy I've heard used to describe this dynamic came from a male friend of mine who is in a soulmate relationship, cheats on his wife regularly but doesn't leave for reasons of friendship, love for his wife and for reasons of finances. *My marriage feels like a warm bath. It's not so hot that I have to get out and it's not so cold that it's uncomfortable to stay in. I'm not completely happy. But I'm not unhappy either. I could be happier and more in love. I could be unhappier.*

Being with our soulmate makes us feel like we're following the rules of success that we've been given for love and life. It feels safe.

We can thank our parents here for shaping our definition of love and what success in a relationship looks like. Not only of what love and family is but sometimes how we plan to do it better for ourselves and our children than what we grew up experiencing.

I can't tell you the amount of people whom I speak to who are holding on in their marriages because their own parents divorced and they don't want that for themselves or their kids.

With soulmate love, both individuals stay the same and don't evolve out of their conditioning too much which is the requirement for this connection to continue in comfort. However, it is as we evolve, through age and life experience, when we start to see soulmates growing and sometimes outgrowing one another.

In this space, the one evolving and outgrowing either curtails their soul growth so as not to outgrow the connection for reasons of love, safety, security, family or finances. Or they leave the connection.

This is where we see individuals trying to keep a lid on their inner world and their feelings of discontent and disconnection to maintain the relationship. This is where someone can accidentally (or purposefully) fall into an affair, or many affairs, either emotional or physical. Their inner world is in turmoil and conflict, whether they have conscious soul awareness of it or not.

Someone here might say 'it was just physical' or 'it didn't mean anything' but I would like to counter with you that neither statement is completely true. Both statements are simply a reflection of their own lack of inner awareness and lack of soul awakening in themselves. There was a soul desire or need behind it—whatever that might have been.

To end our soulmate relationship is to often go against other people's expectations and hopes for us and to break free from what we were supposed to do, often disappointing those we love most in the process.

Leaving a soulmate relationship that is bound by marriage and getting a divorce in the process merely exaggerates all of this. The ties that bind emotionally, socially and in a familial sense run deep.

Soulmate love is safe and feels familiar and it's why some of us have difficulty moving on from this love even when we feel elements of disconnect in the connection.

You can see now why many prefer the comfort of staying comfortably asleep around you. Better what they know than the unknown of what they don't and to potentially disappoint others in the process and lose the love from others around them as a result.

Early on in these relationships we see glimpses of why things won't ultimately work out. But often we are so in our head and in our humanness at the time to be able to fully see past ourselves. And as the relationship progresses, we find ourselves having walked too far down the path of living the dream we once laid out for ourselves to want to now see it or feel we can go back.

These individuals put their blinkers on, closing themselves off to the pull of the soul journey. Staying very much in their humanness and their conditioning.

Soulmate relationships are based on comfort. There is not the sharing of the mesmerising energy ties present in twin flame relationships.

Individuals who choose to leave a soulmate relationship do so because they come to realise that this relationship is holding them back from experiencing the next level of life and love open to them. The price of staying in the relationship begins to feel too personally heavy for them to continue.

If you have left a relationship or marriage to a soulmate, whether by choice or consequence, someone followed their inner voice and their soul to do so.

It has started a soul journey. How you choose to walk it is your path now—still from your point of humanness or from your soul.

The choice is yours.

KARMIC LOVE:
THE LOVES THAT TEACH US THE
LESSONS WE DON'T WANT TO HAVE

*'If your life is going through cycles and repetitiveness
you are not going to reach anywhere; it is time to
change the pattern.'*
— Sadhguru

This is the love we are seeing mostly played out in the modern dating world.

Karmic love is the cause of the car crash present in today's dating sphere.

Souls beginning new relationships before they have actually dealt with the wounds and lessons from their last ones. Souls who are at varying levels of awareness and awakening to the process of growing and evolving through love. All of them, learning on one another as part of their soul evolution.

This is what we call a karmic cycle and it's one that many divorced people find themselves in.

We can experience multiple karmic partners in our lifetime. Not because our one is not out there but because we're not ready for our one.

Perhaps there are other growth pathways that need to be explored in you first. Other lessons for you to master. Elements that when brought together in time will make you into a whole, shining version of yourself first.

Karmic love is a process of ascension.

It is common for us to have as many karmic loves as it

takes until we learn the soul lessons that we need to have. Until we see and heal the voids within our soul. The voids that many of us attempted to fill through our soulmate relationship.

A need to not be alone or be rejected.

A lack of love for ourselves.

Our need to people-please.

Owning our voice and needs. Being comfortable to express them.

A fear of security and not being able to provide for ourselves financially.

Low self-worth.

Lack of confidence and belief.

Our want and hope to be rescued.

Our own emotional unavailability.

A lack of inner grounding, balance and purpose.

Using sex as a way to avoid emotional depth and intimacy.

This is why dating after divorce can both feel and look like a car crash. In many ways it is because so many are still dating from their humanness and ego! They haven't learnt the lesson or are oblivious to the soul journey that is actually shaping theirs and everyone's love choices and behaviours.

Karmic loves teach us that we can't look to another to make us feel better about ourselves or to give us a sense of belonging or self-worth. And there is a steep cost when we try to.

This love teaches us that we have to be strong enough to stand on our own two feet.

This love teaches us the patterns we need to change so

that we can change who we attract, which means we first need to change the energy of who we are and how we move through love and the world.

And it will keep doing this, over and over again, in as many different partners as necessary, until we wake up to the lessons and growth we need to have.

Karmic loves are painful like that.

This love shines a light on the gaps within our soul and because we are in the process of awakening and evolving, this is why we so often project and see these loves as our 'forevers'.

Our 'one.'

We need them to be more than they are.

These relationships are so close to our ideal minus a few red flags that we've downplayed often from the start because everything else was so damn right.

This is the relationship that comes in when we feel we've done enough work, when we feel we've had enough time on our own, when we think we're ready. Only to realise… no, this isn't quite true.

The end of a karmic love relationship is one of the most painful moments on the journey to finding the one because we realise we haven't come as far as we've hoped.

Their ending can literally bring you to your knees.

They mirror back to us how wounded we still are and how much growing we still have to do—not just in terms of our intimate relationships, but also in our personal development.

At a soul-level, this relationship teaches us that there is no way out of self-growth and there is no short cut, as much as we might try.

The effect of the karmic love process cycling through the adult, post-divorce dating pond is significant. It's why many men and women start to feel a sense of hopelessness when it comes to love.

It was so much easier to fall into love and to keep a lover when we were younger. Now it feels like no one wants a relationship and no one wants to settle down. Now we are left feeling that we're not good enough.

Karmic love is the cause of many men and women feeling jaded about love and the dating pool. The hurt from these relationships can be so soul destroying that people give up on love, decide they'd rather stay single, shut off emotionally and even shut off on a soul level and choose to only pursue the physical.

Yet, we must realise this about the love journey after divorce.

The desire to settle down after divorce is different now than it was prior to getting married. Everyone has already left a love that led them to have to compromise, put their needs to the side or that has cost them emotionally, financially and socially—often in painful ways.

Which doesn't mean that an individual is not open to love and settling down again. It just means that they're not willing to do it for anyone. And since we know that looks can capture but don't necessarily hold a soul's gaze forever, this then means that, in order to last, the love connection has to run much deeper than it ever has before.

An individual is going to have to really capture their attention, awaken something within them and stir their soul in such a way that it makes them want to stop swiping, delete the apps, stop looking around for their next option and feel that they have landed on such a love and person that is so unique that they couldn't possibly let it go.

This is not going to be everyone that you meet.

Spiritually, we call this person our twin flame. The one.

Karmic love is an addictive love. Twin flame love is a whole other level. It is magnetic because of the energy they give off and bring out in one another.

Whether someone is awake to the process or not, love after divorce is a soul journey that some will experience consciously or not.

Now you can experience it consciously and not lose hope because you can see it for the process that it is.

Each love is teaching us something. Sometimes painfully, because we so desperately wanted it to work and for them to be the one.

Each love is ascending us higher in ourselves and on our path.

But there is light. The more open and awake we stay to this process of soul growth and alignment, the faster we will ascend through it towards the love that will rock our world, wake us up even further and that will grow with us, over us outgrowing it.

Twin flame love.

Your energetic match.

Cut from the same soul and split in two.

The ultimate power couple in love and life that inspires others around them with their love, sometimes even with their message and the way they choose to live.

These couples exist as the reminder of what is real, true and possible in a loving relationship. Of what we deserve and desire.

Not everyone believes in the concept of twin flames, but I believe it to be true.

I counter that we don't see as many of these power couples in life as we should because not everyone continues to walk this path with an open heart. Many settle and compromise before they find their twin flame. They give up on this love before they arrive. Or they stay in a discontented marriage and choose to not follow the path.

When you leave a marriage, you are choosing this path. You have stepped beyond your fear and conditioning.

Whether you have realised it or not, you are on the soul path.

THE ONE BEFORE THE ONE: THE LOVE THAT WE WANT TO WORK AND THAT SHATTERS OUR SOUL WHEN IT DOESN'T

'It is strange how often a heart must be broken before the years can make it wise.'
— Sara Teasdale

I'm going to slide this one in here, not because they are their own type but because the heartbreak this love leaves us with warrants its own chapter.

The one before the one.

This love is often the precursor to us having a dark night of the soul. A heartbreak that cuts so that deep that it leaves us questioning everything that we thought we knew about love and believed about ourselves.

When it ends, this love can be soul shattering.

The one before the one is known as the false twin flame phenomenon.

The love and attraction is so deep it feels destined, and we so wish it be so that we overlook all the reasons that show us it is not so.

A false twin flame is someone that you believe is your one, but they are not.

You will look back on this love and wonder in time how you ever believed them to be the one and why you ever placed them on such a pedestal.

Hindsight is always humbling with this one.

If drama, arguments, pain, ghosting or cheating occurs in this relationship, if you have been the third person in their life for a period of time without resolve or forward movement, and all of this continues to roller coaster and occur without real positive ascension or progress, then you are not with your twin flame.

You are not.

The entire purpose of the twin flame relationship is soul evolution in both individuals within the connection.

You both inspire one another to grow and develop into the best version of yourselves. If this doesn't happen in both, then no matter how much you might wish, hope or believe it to be so, regardless of how magnetic the sex or attraction you have with this person, you aren't with your twin flame.

It is karmic love. And there are lessons here for you to learn.

Twin flame love connections are rarely straightforward as you will come to understand in the next chapter.

Their entrance into our life always brings with it a shaking to our core and foundations which is why this relationship can be so often associated with less-than-ideal patterns: push/pull dynamics, time together and time in separation while we process the entrance of this kind of love into our life, questioning what we want and what we're ready for and what we're going to do about this love.

A twin flame connection walks into your life and nothing is ever the same again. Even if you're not in a relationship with them.

Such is the effect they will have on you until you come into union with them.

My belief is that we should never give the twin flame label to anyone in our life until they are fully showing up as one.

Up until that point, we should keep evolving forward in our life and self and only give them the label of 'maybe' or 'potentially' until time reveals itself. Like it always does.

We should never keep ourselves available for a connection if it is not treating us like we deserve, if it is costing us our self-worth, respect or confidence simply because we believe them to be our twin flame.

That is us romanticising someone and seeing them for their potential not their reality.

This can be dangerous territory.

That can be us co-creating and choosing toxicity.

The ending of this relationship leaves many devastated and so heartbroken that they choose to stay single for a time. The ending of this love makes us feel that it's easier to stay single and focus on our own life because it's just not worth the pain.

Eventually, after healing, we come to the full realisation that maybe there's more to life than being in a relationship anyway. And in our core, we are deeply comfortable with it.

We begin to more deeply explore all the things that we love and that we are passionate about. The things that bring us soul joy and bring out the best in us.

Us finding and being in our soul alignment.

This love breaks us in such a way that it becomes the catalyst for our twin flame.

Without it, we would never have desired, by our own choice, to deeply examine the parts of ourselves that need healing and opening.

This love breaks us.

But it also makes us.

TWIN FLAME LOVE: THE LOVE THAT MAKES US STOP

'The twin flame union is the strongest, deepest and purest form of love that can be experienced by two entities within this universe. It transcends all other types of bonds and relationships. However, the success of a twin flame union requires that both entities are spiritually prepared, that they are capable of releasing their egos in order to act only out of unconditional love.'
— S.J. Morgan

When we begin the journey of moving on from a marriage, we leave with a sense of hope that the love that will hopefully come into our world after leaving will be better than the one that we've left behind. Very rarely does anyone leave hoping for a similar shade of the same kind of relationship in the future.

Certainly no one leaves hoping for worse.

We all leave hoping that in choosing ourselves we are, in essence, also choosing *for* ourselves and our children a better life that brings us more peace, love, soul freedom, joy and a level of abundance.

Spiritually, a twin flame union is the peak union.

Its entrance into our world will leave us questioning if we've ever even loved before. It makes us see all of our previous love choices for what they were—our conditioning or a choice made from a place of fear.

Twin flames are the same in their soul. They are the one soul split in half. By consequence they have very similar goals, ideas, values, personalities, wants, needs and desires. This is because twin flames are naturally of a higher level of vibration—they have done or are doing the soul work to be at their best.

They are of the same frequency and are of the same energy level.

This is why this love has a magical spark over an addictive pull that we don't see felt in other love connections.

When twin flames first come together, any negative belief about love or self that they carry such as hurt, fear, emotional baggage, shame or negative patterned behaviour all comes to the surface for you to be able to relinquish. It does so because this is a different energy of love than we've ever experienced before. Everything that is not love as a result of the past can't exist here in this union.

All of it comes to the surface to be cleared, and within a twin flame relationship it is cleared, remembering that by definition:

A twin flame connection is the catalyst for positive change and soul evolution in both individuals.

As one soul awakens and heals so does the other.

The entry of a twin flame connection into our life almost always brings with it a level of complication. This is because its entrance into our life is typically much later in life when much of our life, even our mindset, is already set.

Even if we may have met this person earlier in our life, it is unlikely that we will find ourselves in a relationship with our twin flame until later in life. This is because most of us wouldn't have been ready for them any earlier. We were still too much of a product of our conditioning and past wounds. In order to receive our twin flame, we need to have not only cleared a large amount of our karma through previous relationships, but we need to have reached a point of more awareness and evolvement of who we are as individuals.

And so, as a result...

Both individuals have almost always had children already. One or both souls may still be in another relationship or even a marriage. One or both may still be in the energy of their conditioning, of living a life of responsibility and 'I should'. Some twin flames find themselves awakening to their dissatisfaction with it all but having made none of the practical steps to change or end it.

Some twin flame connections are the same sex, from different cultural or socio-economic backgrounds, living in another part of the world, or have significant age disparities.

Your twin flame is, as you can probably tell, often someone you never thought would be your type, who you could have never imagined being your person, who you never expected to end up with or to feel for in the way that you do.

Often our twin flame is far from our conditioned type.

It's not who you were conditioned to bring home to mum and dad.

Even the timing of this love's entrance into your life will not make sense at the time, though it will later with reflection, going on to change everything in your life after it does.

An individual's version of what love actually is will begin to be questioned when the presence of their twin flame enters their life. They will see all that they've settled for and compromised to keep love and family together in the past and the present.

Their values will change and so will their view on what they want from life.

Friendships and relationships will change as they begin to evolve and wake up. Some of these will end.

Some will experience career change.

Or even move cities and countries.

A twin flame's presence into your life truly awakens your soul.

It is a process of awakening to love and self that once started can't be stopped.

And so, their entrance into your life becomes a marker of life before them and life after them because you—and your life—are never quite the same ever again.

From the beginning when twin flames meet, even before they are in a relationship together, they will feel a deep knowing of each other, a comfort level and ease that they haven't felt in quite the same way with another, a freedom and acceptance to fully be themselves and a desire to just be in each other's energy in some way.

True twin flames will always return to one another, there isn't another choice. It is not an addiction. It is a pure desire to be in some way close to their counterpart and in their energy. You can't choose your twin flame or who you want it to be. Your twin flame just is who it is. You are joined on a spiritual level.

As one soul heals and awakens so does the other. The work you do for yourself will always translate to your twin flame's growth too.

You are polishing the diamond that is both of your souls.

Twin flames have divine timing even if it at first doesn't make sense. Despite how hard we might try to deny it. In this connection we receive a glimpse of something that remains on our heart, a connection becomes ignited that always remains.

Your feelings for a twin flame will challenge your rational brain because nothing about this connection is normal or traditional.

As one of my clients so eloquently put it, 'If I leave my

wife for her, it will cost me millions but if I don't do this to be with her, I'll regret it for the rest of my life.'

Rather than healing our past, the growth within a twin flame union is about being able to open up to our future. It's less about who we are and who we were and more about the person we're meant to become.

Twin flames move through various phases that form part of the overall journey. Because they come in so unexpectedly and often later in life, it often means we have to rearrange our lives to make this union happen. In this process of rearranging a life, yours and theirs, know a twin flame will never force you to accept less than you deserve or treat you with narcissism.

But you both will challenge one another during this connection.

This love is defined by stages of progression and seeming regression. Of awakening to the connection and this constant feeling of being drawn to them. Of deep passion and attraction like you've had with no other. Of feeling deeply triggered by what the other mirrors back to us. Stages of pulling away, running and chasing as the depth of the connection causes one or both to pull away, not ready to see or make the changes in their life or selves that is necessary for this relationship to come together. Of surrendering to the union and accepting that this connection is forever instead of trying to fight it—neither has to be afraid of rejection here. All of this transpires before a union and a definitive relationship can occur.

Twin flame love and the way this connection comes together is going to be vastly different than the pathway that led you to be married.

Throw every rule book out that you had about love and

how it might happen for you and how it might look.

Those rules don't apply here.

TWIN FLAME LOVE: REAL OR BULLSHIT?

'Twin flames don't "complete" you because you are already innately "complete" at a soulful level. Instead, they compliment [sic] you deeply and help you to grow.'
— Mateo Sol

Twin flame love is a connection that defies logic and expectations. Until we have experienced this love it is easy to dismiss it as spiritual mumbo jumbo.

You might be surprised to read this, but it actually doesn't matter what you believe here.

Those who have experienced a twin flame connection, or even a false twin flame, already believe in its existence.

And if you don't, that's okay.

Science will tell you that there is no scientific evidence to support this spiritual ideology. I would counter how can science talk about and dismiss the soul journey while it's still trying to understand and capture its entry into our physical human body.

We don't know what we don't know.

And we don't know a lot.

For some who have always applied the rational, logical and the conditioned mind to love, this concept of twin flames, maybe even this concept of the soul as I've described in this book, is going to seem far-fetched.

But your belief or your non-belief here doesn't actually change whether this love exists or doesn't exist.

My only wish is for you to stay awake and conscious to the soul process I've shared here. For you to take your human conditioned blinkers off, to continue living your life and to choose to neither be closed or open to this twin flame concept.

Rather, let's just see what happens for you now that you are aware of the concepts around soulmates, the karmic love cycle and twin flames.

Let's see what you notice now around you. How your perception of others and their behaviour begins to change.

Sometimes just knowing and having the awareness changes and opens up everything.

ARE TWIN FLAMES TOXIC?

A twin flame connection will challenge you, trigger you and mirror back to you everything you need to ascend and rise above. It becomes toxic only when one or both in the connection don't rise above. Which means it's not a twin flame connection... it's karmic.

A twin flame connection is only toxic if you believe and are holding onto someone being your twin flame before they have earnt the label. And accepting and tolerating toxic behaviour in the name of someone being your twin flame is a consequence of this. This behaviour is why the twin flame connection can sometimes be given a bad name. A twin flame love and connection is meant to help you grow and evolve. Yes, it will also shine light on your shadows, wounds and conditioned beliefs that don't serve your highest soul growth.

All of this will trigger you.

But no relationship should ever mistreat you.

Any relationship that does is the invitation for us to step away. Even if you believe someone to be your twin flame this statement still rings true. Remember this connection is a catalyst for you to both ascend and evolve as souls. Not just one of you. If you continue to follow this path, regardless of whether you believe someone to be a twin flame connection or not, then you are always going to be safeguarding yourself by ascending yourself out of toxic behaviour.

So, allow yourself to grow and evolve over holding yourself back. And if they are truly your twin flame, then this will be the catalyst for them to also ascend.

Your growth will ultimately be their growth too.

A REAL-LIFE EXAMPLE OF A TWIN FLAME RELATIONSHIP AND JOURNEY

'If you fall in love with their soul before you touch their skin, it's true love.'
— Anon

One of the more controversial love stories that exists in our modern world is one of the best examples of a twin flame journey running and interplaying itself alongside a soul life path and someone's human conditioning.

Not all twin flame love journeys come with this kind of storyline of course. However, this one is the ultimate cliché and example in almost every way.

When I share this with you it will open your eyes to the conditioning of the human physical world, the societal expectation we are born into and how it so often lies in opposition to the soul journey and knowing that exists within.

It is the love triangle between Diana Princess of Wales, Camilla Parker Bowles and King Charles III. A controversial relationship.

Almost everyone held a strong opinion at one time on this triangular love affair, some perhaps still do. But it is a love story between Charles and Camilla that no one can now deny.

Theirs is a love story that has endured and has been anything but conventional: knowing each other for thirty-five years before they married.

They officially met at a polo match in 1970. Charles was twenty-two and Camilla was twenty-three and they began dating soon after meeting. However, Charles was first in line to be king and, at the time, the royal establishment was not in favour of Camilla or their relationship.

Camilla was known for being a little bit wild—or at least she was according to the royal families exacting standards at that time.

In 1971, Charles joined the Royal Navy, leaving the

country for eight months. Camilla always knew she was not of the expected queen mould, so by the time Charles returned, Camilla had become engaged to someone else, Andrew Parker Bowles. She had moved on and broke Charles's heart in the process.

This is a clear example of conditioning and societal expectations overstepping and rationalising away their connection and their soul desires.

Camilla and her husband Andrew went on to have a daughter and a son, though Charles and Camilla staying friendly throughout. The prince was even named as godfather to Camilla's son.

During this time and in the several years that followed, pressure from the royal establishment and the media mounted on Charles to marry.

In 1980, a thirty-one-year-old Charles began dating an eighteen-year-old Lady Diana Spencer, a virgin who was perceived as the right class worthy of a future king.

Mere months later, Charles proposed to Diana. And months later again they married in front of 750 million people.

The young woman beautiful enough to captivate and step into her future role as Queen Consort.

We saw conditioning and societal expectations from Charles, though likely with a healthy dose of love and affection for Diana also. This was the love he was conditioned to choose and bring home to his family and ultimately the royal establishment.

So, he did.

A soul born into the human physical body of a future king. Imagine that for him.

'The happily ever after' prince coming to save her story. The perfect match and type of catch that someone of Diana's socio-economic background and lineage was conditioned to marry. We saw conditioning and societal expectations from Diana also. I'm sure with a large dose of hope and love also.

Camilla attended the wedding and Diana even then was aware of Camilla's presence in Charles's life. Conscious of the uniqueness of that connection, enough that it stood out to her. In her famous BBC interview with Martin Bashir, Diana was quoted as having 'looked for her' in the church on her wedding day.

She felt Charles and Camilla's connection despite not being consciously aware of why.

Soul love transcends humanness and its conditioning.

Energetically, that must have felt like a threat to someone clutching onto their title certificate of marriage. Clutching onto their humanness and the social construct of marriage as though it trumped the deep love and connection with someone else that just wouldn't die.

In the years that followed, Charles and Diana had two children in 1982 and 1984, William and Harry respectively.

According to Prince Charles's official autobiography, his affair with Camilla didn't start until 1986 once it became clear to him that his marriage with Diana was irrevocably broken. We can only speculate if this is the truth.

Knowing twin flame connections and the magnetic attraction that exists between individuals, either scenario could be true. Both Charles and Camilla clearly tried to repress their soul connection and desire by focusing on the moral obligation of their marriages that they chose based on conditioning until they couldn't deny it any longer.

Diana and Charles went on to separate in 1992 despite it being prohibited for a divorcee to sit on the throne. And at the time due to religious guidelines, Charles would not have even been allowed to remarry.

In 1995, Camilla and Andrew Parker Bowles announced their intention to divorce.

In 1996, Charles and Diana's finalised theirs.

In 1997, Princess Diana was tragically killed in a car accident around the same time that Charles was seeking to legitimatise his relationship with Camilla, a campaign he pressed pause on out of respect for his ex-wife's death— and I'm sure to avoid further public backlash.

In 1998, Charles began to properly introduce the world to Camilla as his partner and to publicly own their love and relationship. They officially moved in together in 2003 before marrying in 2005.

The personal price for Charles to follow his soul desire and longing was huge and why I'm sure it took years for he and Diana to formally divorce and why it took he and Camilla as long as it did to publicly acknowledge their relationship.

Being with Camilla required him to break away from all that he was raised to be and conditioned to know. He went against public opinion, family pressure and royal expectation for their love.

The soul love journey of a twin flame. It knows no bounds. It continues to exist despite all attempts to ignore it.

While we may have opinions about how Camilla and Charles handled their love and how they behaved, we have to acknowledge what we see shining from their every photo together today: a loving couple, steadfast in their support and devotion to one another. Happiness and a deep contentment in their eyes. A supportive and constant presence in each other's lives. Their extended families are now happily ensconced.

Royalist or not, we can say without a doubt that Camilla's presence in Charles's life has supported him to be the best version of himself that he could be at a soul level. And now, the best king that he was born to be.

Everyone loved Diana and wanted them to remain married. The media and the majority of the public despised Camilla. None of it mattered in the end. It never diminished their feelings or connection to one another.

Twin flame love.

The connection transcends all, including controversy and the opinions of others.

HOW TO KNOW IF SOMEONE IS YOUR TWIN FLAME

Society teaches us to settle down with someone.
Twin flame love teaches us to "rise up".
This love is not for settlers but for elevators.

The amazing thing about the twin flame relationship and journey is that it doesn't have to be difficult. Very few of us here have the level of expectation placed upon us like a future king!

Twin flame relationships are of an entirely different energy and an entirely different union. When together, they make love look easy, which often leads one or the other to initially believe that it won't last or possibly continue like this.

Twin flame connections are certainly not one defined by compromise, settling or keeping the peace in the way so many marriages are defined.

The only difficulty we bring and create around our twin flame connection is our desire for it to be in our lives when it isn't or for it to be further along than where it is.

We must see a twin flame for what it is: a love that doesn't follow the same pathway as the previous loves we've known and is ultimately a reflection of the soul work that both still need to do.

Common indicators of the twin flame relationship:
- A knowingness and interest in one another from the first moment of meeting.
- A bond and connection that is unexplainable and unlike anything else you have experienced.
- You are finely tuned to each other's energies and emotions. Intuitively you just know.
- Their presence in your life is a catalyst for you to both grow and evolve positively towards your fullest potential.
- You are a mirror for each other's fears and desires.
- Explosive chemistry and a strong physical attraction.

- Overwhelming feeling of unconditional love. You know they will never judge you or reject you.
- The entrance of their love into your life wakes you up and creates a complete upheaval in your life.
- In the early stages of the relationship, you become scared of the relationship and want to bail.
- You never have to put on a show for them. You can be your authentic self.
- A feeling you have known one another in previous lifetimes.
- Shared values, beliefs, lifestyles and points of view.
- Unconditional love and an understanding of one another.
- You feel a sense of completion and peace in having found each other.
- A desire to be close to one another and to remain in each other's lives.
- Intimacy and friendship on all levels is unparalleled.
- Meeting this person perpetuates a spiritual awakening in both of you.
- Neither of you are ever the same person again for all the right reasons.

As you can see, twin flame love.
It is no ordinary love.
It is entirely unique.

Its existence is disbelieved and doubted by those who haven't discovered it along their life path as yet but believed and accepted by those who have. These are the people who have experienced the magnetic pull and lived the catalytic effect that came with the entrance of their twin flame into their life. Something they never asked for that changed their perspective on life and love quite entirely.

THE STAGES PRESENT WITHIN A TWIN FLAME CONNECTION

'A good relationship is a sharing; there is no dependence.
Both partners remain totally free and independent.
Nobody possesses – there is no need. It is a free gift
– I have so much, so I give it to you.'
— Osho

There are no guarantees or timelines when it comes to a twin flame connection. No 'must happens'. What is always true is that the entry of your twin flame into your life becomes a point of reference in your soul journey—whether you are in a relationship with them or not.

There is the time before your twin flame entered your life. And then there is the time thereafter because nothing in your life is ever the same again.

Their entry becomes a significant reference point in your life. A catalyst for life turning on its head. The beginning of a true waking up to love, life and your soul's potential. And the unstoppable pull of your soul and the life force around you to lead you there. Sometimes you will feel as if it is ordained and even against your will.

There is no falling back to sleep or going back to who you once were. Try as you might. This is the distinction of a twin flame connection—it is a catalyst for positive growth for both individuals. This is inevitable because both have awakened to the elements within themselves and the aspects of life that are not in alignment with them. Neither can go back to living how they did before.

While the twin flame relationship can be intense and difficult at first, they still treat you with love. Love is always present. Love always remains throughout the stages of this connection that I will share with you below.

Be aware of your ego attaching itself to someone who you think is your twin flame when in fact love is not present, does not remain and there is not positive growth.

Twin flame relationship stages:
1. Signs and synchronicities that a big change is coming into your life.
2. The recognition of your twin flame. A desire to be in one another's energy. To be in conversation with one another. A falling for someone harder than you expected or in a way that doesn't make rational sense.
3. Insecurities and triggering of one another. Of old wounds and beliefs. The release of what needs to be cleared in their lives so that life is in alignment for each individual within the connection. The runner and chaser dynamic can happen during this stage as an individual experiences being triggered by life or the other

and as they heal from the changes arising as a result of the connection in their life.

4. Surrendering to the connection. Both stop fighting the connection and the presence of one another in their life, despite the triggering and changes that the connection brings to their life. The full acceptance of this being a unique connection in their life that neither want to relinquish.

5. Healing and growing together. A union. The allowing and settling into an unconditional love for one another. There is no dependence.

6. Oneness. Finding a shared purpose and cause for the two souls that inspires others around them. The power couple.

THE CREATION OF POWER COUPLES

'A twin flame wants what's best for our soul. A soulmate wants what's best for our humanness and theirs.'
— Unknown

What is my desire with this book? What do I wish to awaken within you and to inspire in humanity? The answer: my desire is to create a world that is full of more power couples living at their fullest potential instead of seeing a world full of more mediocre couples. Couples settling for and managing behaviours and circumstances that are not healthy or fulfilling for them.

One of the painful aspects of my profession as a divorce coach is the social conversations that occur when a group of people who I've just met find out what my profession is.

If they're divorced, their response is, 'Oh, I wish I had known about you while I was going through my own divorce.'

If they're married, the response turns almost straight to their own less-than-ideal marriage dynamics and the things they have to tolerate from their husbands or wives. All interjected with self-deprecating humour, of course.

Sometimes I get so tired of having to have these social conversations that I tell a little white lie when asked what I do for work—I tell them I am a dental hygienist (my former profession).

I joke that, socially, I'd rather hear about people's bad teeth than their marriage problems when I'm enjoying downtime! Both professions illicit a sharing of a story in some way!

And while I laugh and smile at the wife complaining about her husband who is drinking too much again tonight, or who is doing this and that, and who isn't stopping despite her attempts to rein him in with dirty looks, the silent treatment or talk of not trusting them to go out again, I am looking at her and wondering something much different.

I imagine where she would be in life and in herself if she wasn't trying to manage and deal with behaviour that she doesn't like and that isn't aligned with her? If she was with someone who didn't do that and behaved instead in a way that her soul desires.

Imagine what potential this woman could reach if she

wasn't stuck in her head so much worrying about how to manage someone's behaviour and trying to keep it all together when he's clearly not caring or all that concerned about it.

Imagine who she could become with more energetic capacity and space to focus on the positive.

Imagine if she just let it go and stopped trying to make him act in the way she needed him to act. If she just let him be who he was at his core and she just let herself be who she was at her core. And if that meant their relationship had to end, then at least they were both free to meet others who were already aligned with who they were and what they valued.

I think this a lot when I meet many couples in a social setting.

Imagine where they would be in themselves if they stopped trying to hold on and control.

PART 4

Lessons to Master on Our Path to Finding Our Twin Flame

SHIFTING FROM A HUMAN/ EGO-LED LIFE TO A SOUL-LED LIFE

'Begin to see yourself as a soul with a body rather than a body with a soul.'
— Wayne Dyer

Leaving my marriage came with so much undoing of my past life and a walking away from it. The selling of the house. The splitting of the possessions. Losing of some friendships. Even my identity changing. It felt like I chose myself and then lost so much of what I loved in the process.

Earlier in the book I talked about the three types of people we encounter during the finding love after divorce journey.

The third being the awake human who is leading and living entirely from the point of their soul. Their physical world and relationships are built around them in such a way that it supports their soul and its growth.

This person is living in alignment with their soul and is in alignment with their twin flame even if they haven't met them yet. Whether they meet them now or whether they will meet them later in their life path, they are in growing alignment with one another.

I want to let you know that this individual didn't miraculously find themselves born into such an aligned space or have it magically appear as an adult.

They purposefully created this aligned life over time.

And that purposeful creation required them to, at many different times, let go of the elements, relationships and parts of their life that were no longer in alignment with their soul and who they were becoming.

Making big changes has felt harder and clunkier the older I get. Including those times when I wanted and asked for the change.

During those moments, the physical world around me felt binding; the weight of change felt heavy. And internally, my thinking, beliefs about myself and concept of right for me and no longer meant for me was shifting.

There were mortgages to consider.

Children to consider.

My living situation to consider.

What sort of work I wanted to do now (and if I was even going to be able to do it well).

Affordability and finances to consider.

Relationships to consider.

Responsibilities to weigh up.

All of these things weighed heavily on me at different points in my journey of changing my life to be one that was soul-led and in alignment with who I really was.

Your own awakening process will happen for you. How far you choose to travel down the path of realigning your life to be more soul-led will be your own personal journey.

However, you choose to walk it, this process always begins with one step. To just start.

Start with your greatest source of pain and frustration in your life and work to create change and evolve forward in that space first. And then begin to slowly start stripping back more and more of the elements of your life that are not in alignment.

If your job is sucking the life force out of you then what could you do instead? If your financial fear is limiting your future choices, then what action can you take to open and improve your mindset? If the place or city you are living in creates financial stress, then do you need to be living there? Is your romantic relationship aligned with what you value and how you feel?

Undoing the physical human ties that bind and keep us trapped and limited from ascending is a life-long process for many.

It's not a race. But it is a place that, once arrived, you can never go back. A place where your world and relationships are in alignment with what your soul desires.

This is why you hear divorced people look at not-so-happily married couples and wonder why and how they are still doing it to themselves.

Once you've ascended out of such a limitation in your intimate relationship, you find yourself too awake to return back to anything less than what is now your new normal.

I don't want to glorify this.

It can be a contrasting journey of both love and loss. This path is not always an easy one to walk. It can be extremely uncomfortable and triggering at points.

But it is a path that, once walked, you never look back on with regret.

You are free in many senses of the word.

You have left the trap that many around you are still living in and trying to make work.

You are free to create a life and love that is meant for you, aligned for you and that is a reflection of who you are now.

CHOOSING TO IGNORE THE SOUL JOURNEY WITHIN

Wherever you go... there you are still!

For most of us, our outer world does not support the soul within. This is a sad reflection of modern society and everything we have valued or been taught to value and prioritise in life up to now.

Souls were not designed to live in the way we are forcing them to live.

Going to work every day to sit in a cubicle or work office, repeating the same tasks today that we did yesterday. Swiping and seeking connection or entertainment, sacrificing ourselves to keep everyone else happy or our finances together. Sharing our bed and our body, our most intimate space, with someone who doesn't even treat us well or love us like we deserve. Chasing the next thing to have or own. Desiring to look a certain way so we feel good enough to others.

You can choose to ignore the inner soul journey as much as you like, but the consequences of doing so will continue to follow you for as long as you do so.

Inner turmoil.

A feeling of disconnect.

Confusion.

A strong intuition that something feels wrong or off.

Depression.

Carrying of excess weight that we are struggling to shift.

Sleeplessness.

These are the rumblings of a soul that is desiring to be heard. When we ignore our soul desire and callings for too long, we go on to experience that age-old mid-life crisis.

A mid-life crisis is someone re-aligning their human life to their soul. A mid-life crisis is someone beginning to listen to the soul journey within without even realising that they are. The individual who walks away from everything they once loved.

Who quits their job.

Sells everything up.

Buys a motorbike.

What are they doing? Who are they?

They are free, is what they are. Specifically, their soul has started to speak and has taken over the reins of their life.

This person feels liberated. Free. They feel happier and lighter than they've felt in a very long time.

They feel younger. And they often look it too.

The weight on our psyche when we ignore the soul journey within is a heavy one. You won't realise it until you drop the human load and start to live and make choices from a soul place.

This is not a shirking of your responsibilities. It is an adjustment of them.

Of course, not everyone is going to agree. Perhaps some of you here have had this happen to you courtesy of your ex-partners.

In this case, we must let them go. It's pointless to judge them or to carry too much resentment for too long. This doesn't erase your hurt or justify their behaviour. Instead, it just leaves you with acceptance.

You might not agree with it. You might not have wanted it, but your ex-partners soul outgrew your connection together as it was. And they couldn't ignore their inner turmoil over it any longer.

Use this as the opportunity for you to now come into alignment with who you really are at a soul level. To reinvent and reimagine yourself for the future. To become your best version of self.

It's very hard, near impossible, to find a love that is aligned for you when you are living out of alignment within yourself.

Alignment and coming home to your soul is everything. It is the new version of modern-day success—to have a life that feels as good on the inside as it looks on the outside.

GRIEF AND LETTING GO TO MOVE ON

'With long-term relationships we grieve the ending.
With short-term relationships we grieve the possibility.
One pain is not greater than the other; just different.'
— Unknown

The death of a potential future dream is often the hardest part to let go of when a relationship ends. This feeling is further amplified when a marriage ends.

No one marries hoping to one day get a divorce. No one stays in a relationship hoping it will end.

The more we are aware of the death of the potential and the possibility and the grief that comes with this loss, the more we can accept and allow our feelings to simply exist.

Often this grief is more about what the relationship could have been, or what we hoped it might be, than what it actually was.

Fighting our emotions is futile. Especially in this space.

There is a process of releasing and letting go that forms part of a relationship ending that we can't gloss over as much as we might try. It inevitably catches up with the individual later if they try to dismiss it.

The same rules of grief that we apply to a loved one dying in our life can be applied to the end of a relationship. This is because it is the sudden absence of someone from your life that was once important to you. Only, they are still living which can sometimes make it harder to accept.

Grief takes time.

You will find yourself missing someone's presence for a time until one day you wake up and realise that you have learnt to live without their presence in your life. And without you even realising that you'd reached this place. Your soul and psyche have accommodated their absence from your life.

And just when you think you have grieved the loss of them and have moved on something will happen that will trigger you to fall back into that grief again.

Healing is not linear. Neither is grief.

Grief, once resolved, eventually leaves us with memories that I hope will be ones that are later laced with gratitude for you in your soul.

You cannot fight grief. Grief is an emotion that we have to allow.

Healing our grief between relationships is an important part of moving on and ascending towards 'the one'. Sitting with grief is where we are forced to face our soul lessons and mistakes, however uncomfortable the process.

When we try to skip and avoid this grief process, we end up carrying our baggage with us into our next relationships. Unresolved. Thus, we almost always repeat our patterns again, this time on someone else, because we haven't had the space to learn and reflect.

Expect grief to come and go for quite some time after a marriage and a divorce ends. Even if you were the one who chose to walk away.

Expect that just when you thought you'd overcome the loss of a person or relationship in your life, something else will happen and make you realise that you have not.

Simply allow the grief and letting go process to be what it is for you.

There is no timeline for grief.

In fact, the grief we feel is often more of a reflection of the depth of connection we felt or amount of hope we held for the future than it is about the length of time that we were with someone.

We elongate the process of moving on if we don't allow grief to be what it is for us.

TRUSTING THE TIMELINE OF YOUR LOVE JOURNEY

*'They'll come out of nowhere. You don't have to go
and buy anyone or try to meet the right people. Usually
when you try to meet the right one, they're always the
wrong one. So don't go searching. Those who go searching
for love only make manifest their own love-less-ness,
and the love-less-ness never find love. Only the loving
find love, and they never have to seek for it.
You draw them in; they come to you.'*
— Neville Goddard

I hear this a lot:

Why hasn't love happened for me yet?

Where is he?

Where is she?

I am tired of the dating world.

Tired of being on my own.

There are many who feel and carry with them a distinct feeling of pain because love has not shown up for them in the world as they hoped.

Yet.

Yet is the word. Remember that.

It doesn't say anything negative about you if you haven't met your one yet.

But it is often a reflection that something necessary at a soul level needs to take place, be completed, mastered or changed first.

Almost anyone could walk outside today or put

themselves on a dating app and find someone for themselves if they wanted to. That is, if you released all of your ideals, values or desires.

I am not advising you to do this. I am, however, asking you to recognise that there is the potential for love everywhere in the world. And your singleness is therefore not a reflection of not being good enough.

Love finds all of us when we are walking on our soul alignment path. When we are releasing what is not meant for us and what we don't love in our lives and are instead filling our life with things meant for us that we do love.

The love meant for us finds our way to us when we are becoming who we are meant to be.

So, if love hasn't arrived for you yet then it is simply a case of it not being the right time for it to have walked into your life.

One day, at the perfect life moment, you will walk around a corner and bump into a soul that you never expected to meet: at your new job that you've just started, at the coffee shop in the city you've just moved to, at a new friend's birthday dinner one night, at the club of the new hobby you've taken up. Or someone who you have never fully noticed in your life before will suddenly be someone that you do notice, and they will notice you too because you've both changed and now your souls recognise one another in a way that they haven't before.

The magic of love.

It shows up when you're not looking for it.

When you don't need it.

When you're happily pre-occupied living life.

Keep walking your soul path.

Keep becoming who you're meant to become and creating a life that reflects the essence of who you are.

And when they do show up, you know as well as I do the story of how this goes.

The timing of their full arrival into your life will be perfect. And you'll both be ready for one another. And with hindsight you won't want to change a single thing about the story of how it all came together for you.

It will all make complete sense.

Replace the pain of absence with trust in the journey, stay in soul alignment and keep having fun along the way.

This is how love finds you.

Release the timeline and the energy of waiting. Embrace that it will happen for you when it is supposed to.

Until then, you deserve to live every moment feeling full, happy and joyous.

FEARING YOU WILL END UP ALONE AND NEVER FIND LOVE AGAIN

'Right before we move to a new higher frequency there is always a tower moment to remove everything and everyone who's vibrations are not a match to where we are going. If a lot is crumbling right now you are making the space for more light to enter. Trust this.'
— Esoteric Ankita

When someone leaves a relationship, by choice or consequence, one of the most common fears I hear expressed is 'will I end up alone' or 'will someone ever love me again?'

The truth is that, yes, you might be alone for a time. Yes, it might take some time for you to find someone who loves you intimately again. You might be alone for a little while. In fact, I hope you are. You might be alone for a time and if you are, you will be fine.

More than fine.

Rather than fearing ending up alone I'd love for you to do the opposite.

I'd love for you to embrace being alone for a time. Knowing it's not forever, it's just for a time. And it means absolutely nothing negative if you don't have a partner for a period of time.

It means only what you say it means.

I'm on my own because I'm too old and no one wants me.

I'm on my own because all men/women are (insert your favourite belief here).

I'm on my own because no one wants me.

None of this is actually true.

It means nothing negative about anyone.

If there is one thing I wish I'd done differently since leaving my marriage in 2016, it's that I wish I'd embraced and enjoyed being on my own more than what I did. Instead of fighting it and trying to fill the space.

I wish I'd just allowed it and seen it for the gift that it was. When we fight our loneliness and try to fill the space because it's uncomfortable or triggering, we can let people slip into our life, relationships and energies that in time end up reminding us why we'd have been better off staying on our own!

Finding peace in being alone is essential to you discovering who you are. And for some of you here that is a necessary part of your soul journey.

It took me five years to discover who I was, and I discovered this through time being in a relationship and through the contrast of time being 'on my own'.

Only I wasn't on my own and without love. I might not have had a partner in my life, but did I have love in my life?

Yes of course I did. I had it everywhere.

From my daughters. From my friends. From my family. From myself. From my work colleagues.

Love is everywhere.

Being alone is only ever a problem when we equate it to meaning something negative or less than about ourselves.

And that is a BS narrative. I don't even need to know you to know that this is not true about you.

You being alone does not mean you will be alone forever.

You being alone for a period of time isn't something to fear.

Trust your journey, please.

STAYING ABOVE THE CAR CRASH THAT CAN BE THE DATING POOL

Reacting the same way keeps you bound to the lesson and you remain in this karmic loop. When you are presented with the same situations over and over, you have to do something different. The karmic cycle ends when you decide to no longer participate. When you change your patterns and responses. Then you break the chains and ascend higher, faster. Until then... you cycle.

Yes, the dating world after divorce is a bit of a car crash.

The modern dating world after divorce is a heightened karmic love cycle of the three types of souls we talked about previously in this book.

Souls leading from their humanness and ego. Completely asleep to their soul journey and the lessons they need to have. These people are looking to fulfill their physical needs, ego desires and for a love or someone to make it all better so they don't feel alone or not unworthy.

Individuals awakening to their soul and leading from varying levels of their soul and humanness. They are conscious of the lessons they need to have; they try to overcome unhealthy patterns.

And individuals leading from their soul. Awake and conscious. Not healed, no one is ever perfectly healed, but when a cycle presents, they see the lesson, they ascend.

The modern dating world is mostly full of the first two types of people.

These are the individuals who don't want to be on their own because they would then need to sit with their inner world and all that they're avoiding. These people are looking for love to make them feel better about themselves, to make their life feel more whole, to make them feel enough.

The best way to avoid the pitfalls of the modern dating world is to avoid being one of these individuals.

You've already settled to keep love in your life before. You've already compromised for love to the detriment of yourself in the past. Decide that you have no desire to do that to yourself anymore.

And don't!

And be comfortable to not do so.

This is you making a deliberate decision to choose quality over quantity and to be comfortable with the larger spaces of time that can come with making that choice.

Several years ago, I chose to stay single, deliberately, for a year. It was the first time I'd ever been single without a person or a lover for that long in my adult life.

No one in my bed and no one in my head. It was deeply uncomfortable in many ways and brought up a lot of the self-doubts that I had within myself—to have no one choosing me or chasing me.

During that time, I had a close girlfriend who was also single. During the twelve months of my deliberate singleness, she cycled through six short-term relationships.

Who do you think came out better, entirely different version of self after those twelve months? And who do you think came out of those twelve months as the same person as she went in? If anything, a little bit more wounded for all of it.

You already know the answer.

Stay above the car crash and make the deliberate choice to not be in it. This requires you to have more of an observer's role to the dating world and process. To only dip your toe in if someone is aligned with your ideal.

To see others for the karmic lessons that they are experiencing and need to have without judgement. Lessons that you don't need to have or that you don't want to get caught in again and be forced to relearn.

Staying out of the car crash that is the dating world is you removing yourself from the karmic cycle of other people's lessons and choosing to learn yours in a less traumatic fashion until you meet someone worthy of your time and energy.

If you are dating because you are lonely, know that you can choose to add trauma upon trauma by filling your void of loneliness with a physical body of someone else OR you can go out and fill your life with people and experiences that will make your life feel fuller and more meaningful.

You can be single, looking for love and not be in the car crash. It's a choice to not be in the car crash and to observe others that are.

My advice as an awakened soul is to stay above it. You will only ever set yourself back every time you dive back into it in a moment of loneliness and desperation.

You can't avoid the karmic lessons that you need to have. But you can choose the way you get to learn them! Choose them kindly for yourself.

COMING TO LOVE FROM A PLACE OF 'FIX ME', 'SAVE ME' OR 'MAKE ME FEEL BETTER ABOUT MYSELF'

'People who know their worth cannot help but emit
"love me well or leave me alone" energy. They only
allow real connections with people who are emotionally
ready because they know relationships take a certain
degree of maturity to work.'
— Yung Pueblo

There is much that can go wrong when we come to love from a of void. Have you learnt this post-marriage? This is not to say that we can't ever come to a relationship from a place of need. Of course we can.

But.

And it's a big one.

If you are coming to a relationship from a place of having a person prop you up emotionally, financially, in your confidence or in any other way, then we are avoiding doing that inner work and embodying that growth for ourselves; we are outsourcing and using someone else to embolden us.

And the danger is that if the love from this person leaves our life, then it can deeply shake our emotional and financial stability or confidence.

It leaves you again very vulnerable in a relationship because you are not coming to a relationship from a soul-empowered, whole place. And for many of us who have left a marriage, we have already learnt the price of coming to a relationship from a place of 'fix me', 'make me feel safe' or 'make me feel better about myself'.

The dynamic that was once the attractive hook at the start became the trap that eventually made us fear leaving the relationship. A relationship should add to us becoming the best version of ourselves possible. It is the cliché of two whole people coming together in a relationship. Both in a great space within themselves. Both are of the energy that is 'love me well or leave me alone'.

This is a very different tone of relationship that we often see associated with the opposite energy of 'love me badly but I still won't leave you'.

My personal and professional experience is that it will take most of us several versions of both kinds of relationships to evolve us into the space where we are ready for our twin flame.

The ultimate best version of ourselves is revealed to us through time. It is through the contrast of having poor and great relationships that realigns us onto our soul path. This happens over time until we meet that someone whom we won't outgrow.

The invitation to meeting the one sooner is to ensure you are always coming to every relationship as whole as possible in that moment in time.

Embody the energy of love me well or leave me alone.

And embrace a relationship for as long as it encapsulates this energy.

HOLDING ONTO SOMEONE BELIEVING THEY'RE YOUR ONE

'Attachment to a person or an outcome has its roots in fear and in a need to control or hold onto the familiar. When you allow other people to be themselves you become an excellent parent, boss, lover or friend. Detachment allows the universe to create a perfect result and it is the key to happiness and wellbeing.'
— Unknown

One of the most common things I see in my clients is the above. Holding onto the love and connection with a particular person despite their less-than-ideal behaviour toward us. We hold onto a person who has left us believing or hoping that they will come back wanting us, ready to be the person we wanted them to be, what we originally saw in them.

There is no faster way to keep ourselves stuck or prevent our souls from evolving forward than to approach love from this space of holding onto someone who is no longer meant for us or good for us.

I say this without judgment. I have been here myself and betrayed myself in the process.

The one who got away.

Walking away from someone even though you still love them.

When we stop holding onto someone and start walking forward, what are we really doing?

We are putting ourselves before our love for another.

This is us saying to the constellations through our actions that I love myself more than I love someone else.

I love myself more.

I love myself more.

Just saying those words is realigning and affirming for our soul. It is an invitation to return all of our power back to ourselves, to let go and to detach from the outcome. Detachment allows the universe to create a perfect result.

What is not meant to stay in your life will leave your life, regardless of how much you manipulate or twist to try and keep it in your life.

What we are doing here when we don't let go? When we manipulate, twist or try to create an outcome. We are choosing to delay the inevitable for another time. We are pushing it back further down our life path to have to face another day.

As one of my clients said to me when I asked her, 'If you'd been more confident in yourself in the past when should you have left your ex-husband?'

Her answer, 'Twenty-two years ago when I first caught him out.'

Keep growing and evolving, releasing along the way what isn't aligned for you because it doesn't treat you right, feel right or because it doesn't align with your values or your soul.

Sometimes the people we love so dearly wake up only once we've left them. This is their journey to walk, not yours. And it will be their journey to fix the problem or make their way back into your life if they wake up and realise their misstep—again, not yours.

And it will be your free will as to whether you choose

to go back or realise you have evolved out of the necessity for the relationship.

Rarely does someone wake up to a love lost and the changes they need to make while the love is still so readily available to them at a lower level of vibration.

Embody the energy of the love you desire to have in your life even if it is not in your life yet and keep walking your soul path that is aligned with this.

The beautiful double win of approaching love and life in this way? What's meant for you will level up and return back to you because they couldn't not have you in their life and you in theirs.

What's not meant for you will fall away.

And over time, either way, you will have continued further along your soul path and found yourself having evolved into something else even more wonderful, with them or with someone even better for you.

When that happens, you won't look back or want to go back to how things were. You will have evolved into a whole lot more.

The result will be perfect however it falls.

ATTACHED MORE THAN YOU ARE IN LOVE?

'Attachment gives you more pain than it does love.'
— Priyesh Bharkhda

There is this slippery slope that we so often see in long-term relationships and marriages where the behaviour that is currently happening now is something we would never have accepted or said yes to at the start of the relationship. But here we are, however many years later, settling for it or trying to manage our emotions and lives around it.

It is the frog in hot water analogy; put a frog into a vessel filled with water and start heating the water slowly over time. As the temperature of the water begins to rise, the frog adjusts its body temperature accordingly. The frog keeps adjusting its body temperature with the increasing temperature of the water. Just when the water is about to reach boiling point, the frog cannot adjust anymore. At this point, the frog decides to jump out but it is unable to do so because it has lost all of its strength in adjusting with the rising water temperature. Very soon the frog dies.

What killed the frog?

Many of us will say the boiling water. But the truth about what killed the frog was its own inability to decide when to jump out, before the water became so hot that it was paralysed.

For people in love this looks like us being able to see and accept the relationship for how it is now rather than how we want to see it.

It is a sad truth for us to recognise that how soon we decide to call it in situations like this is actually a reflection of someone's level of self-worth, self-trust in themselves and confidence.

Those with high self-worth, self-trust and confidence would have called it earlier or tried to circumvent this rise in temperature much sooner, as the uncomfortableness began to set in.

They would have seen the writing on the wall much sooner so to speak. As Emma Thompson, an English actress who caught her then-director husband having affairs with other women on set, said, 'What I learned was how easy it is to be blinded by your own desire to deceive yourself.'

Those with low levels of self-worth, self-trust and confidence, even those who also hold deep fears about jumping out and leaving, will adjust their expectations, values and ideals and continue to keep doing so even as the situation becomes more and more uncomfortable.

We all need to adjust with people and situations, but we also need to be sure when we need to adjust and when we need to move on.

There are times when we need to face the reality that we are in a relationship more because of a past attachment to a person than because of how they treat us today and to take appropriate actions from that place.

If we allow people to exploit us physically, emotionally, financially, spiritually or mentally, the sad truth is that some people will continue to do so.

Would I love this person in the same deep way if they showed up in my life today as a stranger and treated me how they're treating me now? If they made me feel about myself like I do now? Made me question myself like I am now?

If your answer to this question is a 'no', then we have some soul path adjusting to do. You are more attached to how someone was in the past than you are in love with who they are now.

This is dangerous territory that will cost you your soul evolution, growth and happiness if you don't allow yourself to ascend out of it.

EXPRESSING YOUR NEEDS
AND TRUTH

*'Let's normalise asking questions for clarity instead of
moving based on the story you've created in your mind
which may or may not be true. Let's normalise expressing
our feelings in healthy ways. Clarity preserves healthy
relationships. And it will bring to an end sooner those ones
not meant for us anymore.'*
— Unknown

Keeping the peace, biting our tongues and not speaking our truths are behaviours I see present in the current marriages and past marriages of many of my clients. If not from them, then from their partner/ex-partner. But typically, both have danced around these behaviours.

A healthy level of compromise is always present in a relationship. However, what I see are many marriages continuing to survive and exist because one if not both are deliberately not sharing their full truth and are more intent on keeping the peace than creating real peace (which costs them their inner peace). This approach never improves a relationship. It simply enables it to continue on forward in the same manner.

Learning to express our needs and our truth after we leave a marriage is a block to overcome for those who survived the constraints of their marriage by learning to bite their tongue and by learning to not express their needs and instead bottle them up.

A healthy relationship with unconditional love can

embrace the expression of your needs and truth when conveyed from a place of love. This will require you to learn how to express your needs and to do so comfortably. To share and talk with honesty. To learn not to just automatically tell someone what you think they want or need to hear.

Clarity and truth in a relationship allows the relationship to maintain a beautiful level of openness and connection that will not only transform and maintain your emotional connection together but also your sexual and intimate connection.

Open communication, a foundation of truth and honesty and learning to express our needs are the pathway to this.

OVER-FOCUSING ON LOVE AND FINDING A PARTNER

'Before you start running after anything, the most fundamental thing is to close your eyes, get in tune with yourself, with your energy, and listen to it—and whatsoever it says is good for you. Then you will find fulfillment. By and by, you will come closer and closer to your blooming.'
— Osho

Why does an individual do this?

Why are you doing this?

I know for many of us after ending a marriage of many years that the thought of being on our own feels overwhelming, triggering and uncomfortable.

We have become so used to being with someone that we can't imagine doing life on our own. Moreover, we might not want to.

One of my biggest soul evolutions was when I was able to reach a point of deep recognition where I could say, hand on heart, that if I never had another relationship in my life that I'd still have lived a full, happy life full of love, adventure and amazingness.

When I reached this point of evolution what do you think happened?

I stopped looking.

And I got on with the business of living a full, happy life full of love, adventure and amazingness in the present.

What do you think happened then?

You already know the answer because it is so obvious and cliché.

I stopped looking from a place of need and from seeking love outside of myself. And I started to over-focus on me and on my own soul path. I found peace in the moments of aloneness. In fact, moments of aloneness became fabulous.

I released all of the things and people that didn't bring peace and joy and brought into my life more of the things that did bring peace and joy.

I embraced every soul lesson that I needed to have to move myself forward instead of hoping that someone would magically enter my life and save me from having to learn it. This allowed me to embody it for myself. Financially and spiritually.

All of this created a deep level of contentedness and alignment in my life that brought with it a knowingness that I was on my soul path where time would bring the right person to me at the right time.

If I had over-focused on love, I would have done so to the detriment of myself, to my own growth and to my own soul path.

I would not be who I am today.

If you stopped looking for love and instead threw all of your anxiety about being single into yourself, where would you be in yourself today?

I would suggest much further along.

EMBRACING THE SEASON YOU'RE IN

'Healing does not require us to become anything new but rather un-become everything we are not.'
— Medicine Mami

One of the beautiful energies of working with a coach like myself is my ability to look at my clients and see quite clearly where their focus and attention needs to go in this moment in time. It is almost always something they don't want to or can't see for themselves. And sometimes not the area of life that an individual comes to me seeking clarity and support on.

There is what we want and think we need. And then there is what we should want and actually do need to evolve us further in life and towards love.

I shared with you that when I left my marriage all I

was seeking was to find love again. That was my desperate desire and soul need. And I did find love again, of course, but it was a love that I continued to keep outgrowing. And why? Because I wasn't who I was meant to be and who I was evolving into. Every relationship was a buffer for everything I was avoiding and not wanting to face within me. For me, being in my marriage took me further away from who I was not. I find this a very common scenario for the individual in the marriage who was of the softer, less dominating energy in the relationship. I morphed myself to fit into the container of the relationship and I lost myself in the process.

Finding myself again was my season.

If you stopped looking for love and instead focused on the other areas of your life that needed your attention, knowing that love will find you while you are living your soul path, what can you see is the season of life that you're living right now? Is it to find yourself again? To find your feet? To thrive in your career? Feel confident in your finances and find independence? Is your life calling you to move or relocate?

Un-becoming after a marriage ends, even when a long-term relationship ends, is a necessary process for some.

Some are ready to dive straight back into a new relationship soon after a marriage ends because they are already living in alignment with who they already are and were meant to be. They were that person already in their marriage.

That was not my journey.

My season involved coming home to me.

It meant learning to express my needs and discovering what I wanted for myself as a single woman now that I no longer had a man in my life defining me and telling me what we were going to be doing or who I needed to be.

It involved entirely changing my career to what it is today. Moving cities. This was something I'd been wanting to do for sixteen years prior, but that my marriage didn't allow.

And there was so much more.

Please embrace the season that you're in and the necessary growth needed for that season. Resisting it doesn't change the season you're in.

In fact, when we embrace it, we allow more peace to join us on the journey. We allow ourselves to walk the path with more grace and ease.

What you will discover is that every lesson learnt and embodied that you pass through leads you to the next in a very straightforward manner.

You can't run before you learn to walk. That old adage rings true here. You can't be further along than where you are right now until you master where you currently are.

This is us taking more of a bird's-eye view to our lives where we recognise why we need to do this and that before we could ever find ourselves ready and an energetic match for our one.

Remember our fate and soul destiny never changes.

All that we have control over is our free will. And our free will can either keep us on the path or take us off the path. It will speed up or hinder the ascension process.

Embracing the season that you're in speeds up the ascension process to you living life as your best self where the one will eventually find you.

Happily loving life already, open hearted and ready.

OVERCOMING YOUR CHILDHOOD AND ITS IMPRINT ON YOUR PSYCHE

'Watching your parents have a dysfunctional relationship is a traumatic experience most people call normal.'
— Dr Nicole LePera

Who were you before life and your childhood happened to you?

We can have a traditionally normal upbringing with supportive and loving parents and still find ourselves walking into adulthood needing to unpack and undo the imprint our childhood has left on our psyches.

The humanness of life intruding on the soul from the moment we leave the womb. We go from a warm environment of peace, muffled noise and nurturing to noise, bright lights, a stranger's touch, pricks on the heels to be jabbed and injected with this and that, and now having to work for our food, love, attention and affection.

No wonder most of us come into the world screaming and crying!

If we were born into an under-nurturing or abusive environment then we can definitely look to our parents and wish they'd been better, more evolved and loving parents.

For better or worse, with all that they knew, your parents did the best that they could with you. As adults, most of us can say this with love in our hearts towards our parents.

Overcoming our childhood is us realigning ourselves with our soul and our soul path before life and the world happened to us. Shaping us to become who we thought we needed to become. To survive. To receive love.

Sometimes who we became as the result of our childhood and the patterns and behaviours we took on are not a reflection of who we actually are on the inside. It might, for instance, support the dynamics and needs of the family unit, but actually, if we reflect a little, it might not have fully supported who you were then or even now.

Your role as an individual that you took on within the family and carried into adulthood for yourself may be holding you back and impacting your path today as an adult.

The best example I can share with you here is myself.

I am the eldest of three children. My mum was nineteen years old when she had me. And I later went on to be the eldest of four children. My mum re-partnered when I was fifteen and had my half-sister.

What did my human experience shape me to become?

As the eldest and only girl with two younger brothers for the early years of my life, I took on the role of the responsible one. I helped Mum a lot. I helped my brothers. I learnt how to read between the lines of what someone needed and the emotions of my home because emotions weren't always communicated.

When my parents fought, they gave each other the silent treatment for days. They liked to break the ice by going to a friend's place for coffee. We'd drive to their friend's house with neither of my parents talking in the car and we'd drive home with them acting mostly normal again.

As a child, I made the smart, right and good decisions. And I didn't miss a thing that my parents tried to hide or thought they were doing a good job of hiding.

I became the perfectionist. The natural over-achiever in school and sport. I won every running race. Made state teams. Always got As on my tests. And my family and friends began to expect it of me.

Carla always won everything.

I started to identify with it too and expect it from myself.

Anything less than first was a failure to me.

I became such a perfectionist, so hard on myself that I transferred it onto all of the other areas of my life and at fourteen I was hospitalised into an adult mental health institution where I stayed for six months with anorexia. At 5'9, I weighed 30 kilograms.

If I was going to have anorexia, even then I was going to make sure that I did that well too. Such was the perfectionist mindset. A+ at being an anorexic.

But why did I do this to myself?

Because underneath the role that I took on as the eldest child, responsible, high achieving, smart daughter who strived and thrived, who was serious and helped everyone, I was actually someone else in my soul. I was highly sensitive, perceptive, empathetic and deeply intuitive. I was creative. I was silly, sweet and fun. I was shy.

My childhood and my family role, accidentally, did not support my soul.

I overcame anorexia but battled with depression and obsessive-compulsive disorder for many years after.

From the moment of recovering from anorexia I literally let go and I stopped trying and pushing myself so hard. I released all need to be the best. I stopped all competitive sports. I settled for Bs and whatever else in my grades.

And because I'd come so close to killing myself because of my striving, no one in my social circle or family ever brought up my lower grades or the disappearance of my competitive nature.

There's no louder message than to sit in front of your loved ones as a skeletal form to let them know *I'm not happy and this isn't working for me*, and for them to adjust their parameters and expectations for you as result...

However, I continued to hold onto the role of the responsible one in the family. I lost all attachment to needing to achieve. I went to the University of Melbourne on a full scholarship that I somehow managed to attain for myself without applying for it. I went from over-achiever to someone who kept having things fall into place for her without too much effort. I chose for myself a smart job as a dental hygienist. I chose the profession solely based on the income I knew I'd earn once I graduated.

I ignored my creativity. I ignored my natural ability to read and see through people and their behaviours. I ignored my inbuilt desire to connect with and help people.

I chose my marriage from the place of being who I thought I needed to be, a success in life and to receive love. He was smart, attractive—a good choice on many levels. Though I didn't recognise it at the time, for me, leaving my marriage freed me to be who I really was.

I just felt so free.

I find this to be true for many men and women after their marriages end.

Leaving a marriage opens allows someone to recalibrate their values, their life direction, even their sense of purpose that their marriage didn't permit.

I lived for thirty-five years as one version of self that the human world had propelled me to take on, over and above my soul desires. It took me the next five years after that to undo the thirty-five years before to reach a point where my life was designed around and supporting my soul in my relationships, friendships, career and lifestyle.

My invitation to you here as you explore the imprint that your childhood has had on your psyche and on your choices is to find for yourself a picture of you as a child. You at an age where you were beautifully innocent and completely you before the world began to change and shape you into who you needed to be. Putting shields around your heart. Taking on a role. Closing your voice out of safety or so you weren't seen as this or that.

Who were you?

What did you love doing?

What words would you use to describe yourself then?

If you hadn't had the family dynamic you did, who else could you have become?

I'd like to suggest that underneath your adultness you still have that same soul energy and essence today that you had as a child. It's just hidden under layers of responsibility, people pleasing, self-abandonment, fear, striving for success, or whatever else.

My request is that you start becoming and taking on the energy of the words that landed on your heart when you looked at the photo of yourself as a child.

That is who you are underneath it all, and the sooner we can have you as an adult, living from this essence, the sooner we will have you again on your soul path.

Who you always were before the world happened to you.

WHEN YOU KEEP ATTRACTING A TYPE

Instead of just labelling someone as emotionally unavailable, toxic or narcissistic, become curious about why you were an energetic match to that person in the first place.

This chapter could also be called why you keep pursuing A type! Because it's never solely a question of who or what we attract. We attract all sorts of people into our everyday world. It's who we choose from within what we attract that speaks volumes.

And it says as much about us as it does them.

It's a hard truth to swallow.

The lessons never come from labelling someone. The lesson always comes when we reflect back on ourselves. This never means we are at fault or the cause of another's behaviour. But we do have to own that we were at one time attracted to them and to our past lovers and partners. Our personality helped enable them to some degree.

Understanding the 'why' to that question reveals everything about us and our inner workings.

If you are:
- Meeting and attracting the same kinds of partners on repeat.
- Having continually bad dating experiences.
- Finding it difficult to trust, be vulnerable and find yourself expecting the worst or seeing the worst in the opposite sex.

Then we haven't dug deep enough on this why and healed the parts of ourselves that need love and attention.

There is something even deeper than we realise that is shaping our choices and perceptions.

This is a life hurdle to overcome on your path to finding the one that many of us have to face at one point in time.

Many of us spend too much time analysing the toxic, emotionally unavailable, narcissistic person and not enough time asking, 'why were they attracted to me?' or 'why did they think they could even try it on with me?'

We are never to blame for the way someone has treated us. We never asked for it. This is not us shaming ourselves either. But there was something about you that attracted them to you.

They have a type too.

And it was you…

PUTTING YOUR DESIRE FOR A CONNECTION WITH SOMEONE ELSE ABOVE YOUR LOVE FOR SELF

'The red flag is when you try to change someone into who you want them to be rather than listening to your intuition saying that they aren't a good fit for you.'
— Robin Clark

There are things we do for love and to keep love in our lives, sometimes to the point of self-ruin and self-sacrifice.

I see many men and women embodying the opposite of

love me well or leave me alone. Instead, their energy and behaviour says: love me badly and I still won't leave you. It's a dangerous dynamic that we create and perpetuate when we allow someone to treat us in a way that is less than how we deserve. When compounded over years within a marriage because we signed on for a lifetime... you can see why many marriages are what they are today.

As you know, I am not anti-marriage or long-term relationships.

I also don't believe that there is no room for mistakes in marriages or long-term relationships either. Of course there are. But the energy 'love me well or leave me alone' says, to me, 'I'll bring you my best self knowing you are bringing me your best self'.

It's a reflection of our self-worth.

Of growth.

Of a desire to keep growing and loving with one another.

A recipe for honesty and emotional maturity.

'Love me badly and I still won't leave you.' If you are carrying yourself with this energy then you won't make anyone rise up in love or allow them to leave your life so you can find someone who will.

In fact, you might even fight and resist them ever leaving you.

Love me well or leave me alone.

No relationship should make you self-compromise to a point of less than what you deserve.

It is your beliefs about yourself and around the availability of love in your life that are stopping you from owning this energy.

LETTING GO OF A LOVE THAT HAS COME TO AN END IN YOUR LIFE

'When you sense it's time to step away from a relationship that's no longer serving you, repeat the following with intent: I am grateful that your soul crossed paths with mine and I appreciate the life lessons we've shared. Even though it's time to move on I wish you blessings on your journey and I am ready to receive whatever comes next. Thank you.'
— Dolores Cannon

One of the hardest things we can do on our love journey is to let go of someone in our life and to release them from our head because we know that our love has come to an end. Grieving the loss of someone who is still alive and maybe not missing us like we are them is emotionally devastating.

But this is necessary work on the path to finding our one. We must let go of love that we've outgrown because it's no longer meant for us or because it isn't treating us like we deserve. I always ask my clients to view moments like this from several points of perspective. Let go of any potential future presence of this person in your life.

Let go of it all.

The potential future dream. How they might wake up to themselves if you just stay around and make yourself available.

Instead, embrace what they have given to you in your life and what they graced you with fully accepting that this is all they are capable of giving you right now.

Perhaps you have hope that someone will return to you one day.

I want you to realise this: in life we never want to go backwards.

So, even if they do make a reappearance into your future, we cannot want them back in our life as the same version of who they were, just as you cannot be exactly who you were.

This relationship ended for a reason.

If they come back into your life as the same person with the same dynamic, you will only end again.

Why go through the exact same dynamics again, having the same arguments or disappointments only to find yourself with the same result?

It is naivety to expect a different result with the same personality, patterns and behaviours.

No, if they return back in your future, both of you will need to be slightly different, more evolved versions of yourselves than you were previously for the relationship to be better.

Both of you will have needed to have woken up to something and evolved as a result of it.

We never go backwards on our soul life path.

We are either repeating the same patterns and lessons again and again until we learn them or we are moving forward.

Let go of that person and of that version of your love together. Be grateful for what it has shown you and stay open.

Open not to a particular person, but to the type of love you desire to experience next—whoever might walk into your life or back into your life and be the person who provides it for you.

MANAGING CONTROLLING AND MANIPULATIVE EXES WHO CONTINUE TO TRIGGER YOU AND IMPACT YOUR LIFE

'When you see someone who needs power and control over you and will not stop until they get it, you are actually seeing someone who is deeply afraid of life. Fearful people can only have things their way.'
— Unknown

Have you woken up to the realisation that leaving a controlling, emotionally manipulative partner doesn't necessarily bring an end to that dynamic?

You've left the relationship but here you still are. Still dealing with the same BS from them. Maybe even worse than when you were together.

I want you to know that this situation is going to more than likely be an ongoing situation for you to manage. Sadly, the only full relief that you may ever experience from it (or at least close to) is going to be when you have a new partner who is fully present in your life and whom you live with.

Your ex will continue to be an ongoing reminder that at one point in your life you didn't express your needs, your boundaries, and your self-love and sense of self-worth weren't quite what they should have been. And they will continue be the presence and lesson of a reminder that you need to embody and master this element within you as part of your soul journey.

We have to manage this scenario in our lives knowing that we can control only ourselves and our self-growth. And by doing so, we can help bring out more of the positive or negative aspects within a person.

**We must take full ownership of the situation
we are in.**

At some point in the past this person was attractive to us and we were attractive to them. If they are controlling, arrogant and manipulative now, then they certainly were, even if in just little ways, in those early days when you met. Yes, they might have worsened over the years but if we look critically at ourselves there was almost always evidence of this behaviour at the start. We just chose to overlook it.

I liken this to the bully in the playground scenario to help us understand. The bully knows how to pick out the other child in the playground who he can push around and try it on with. He can pick up on the energy of the child who maybe isn't all that confident, who is having a less-than-ideal or nurturing time at home. He does all of this without realising.

We know this phenomenon to be true because so often if you move the child who is being bullied out of one school and place him into another school what happens? They are bullied again only in a different environment.

How is this relevant to this situation? We must own what once made us attractive to a person who likes to be in control, be dominant and will manipulate to get their own way and to remain dominant and in control. And we must do the deep inner work to resolve all of what asking that reflection reveals about us.

The lacks and the voids and the beliefs we held about ourselves that their personality made up for at that time. All the facets that we're now paying for.

Be like a grey rock.

When we are in a conversation or situation with someone who is trying to trigger us emotionally so that we doubt ourselves, stay the same or feel inferior (enter your own personal situation here, but this person often has a superiority complex), I always ask my clients to be like a grey rock.

Be bland with your answers. Let your answers be even tempered, cool, calm and collected and not reactive. Present the facts and don't colour or embellish or add emotive language to the situation when you're in conversation. Be as boring as you can be with your replies and don't bite. And however they react, stay in the same vibration of being a boring, grey rock.

Understand that this person is often naturally more combative than you are. They probably even get a bit of a rise out of it all. So don't even try to out-win them in this arena. Refuse to participate in it.

Know your worth. Hold your ground. Stay true to the outcome or intention you hold for the situation. Be a grey rock.

Recommit to yourself.

I made a commitment to myself when I left Perth that I was never again going to tolerate emotionally manipulative or controlling behaviour from anyone in my life ever again. I'd already drawn a line under it but this was the firmest, hardest line that I'd ever drawn in my mind. It was an absolute, I'm-not-buying-in-to-it-anymore decision.

There's a difference in drawing a line in the sand and drawing an absolute line in concrete.

This recommitment is going to be important for you into the future.

Because if you have children with an ex-partner who is bringing this dynamic into your life when they are triggered, then know that you are more than likely going to experience future reoccurrences of this dynamic whenever they see fit.

When you are progressing or moving forward in your life, doing something they don't agree with or want. If they feel they are losing control or superiority over you or the situation.

This situation is going to take a lot of resilience, confidence and a sense of empowerment greater than you potentially hold now. I want you know that you can eclipse this dynamic and rise above it. And rise above it again when you need to in the future.

It will take skills that you might not have now and a vision for your future grander than you have possibly created for yourself in this moment. But this is the pathway to rising above it.

We should never allow ourselves to be pushed around

emotionally by bullies, whether we are in the playground as a child or elsewhere as adults.

Ultimately, it is us who decides when we will no longer tolerate it. When we draw a line of 'no more' on it. When we decide to stop tip-toeing around or trying to keep the peace with someone who is intent on bullying and manipulating us.

Please note: I don't apply this advice to situations of domestic violence. Please seek professional support for yourself in this environment.

SITUATIONSHIPS AND NON-COMMITTAL LOVERS: WHAT TO DO WITH THEM

'When the chase ends, the responsibility begins.'
— Lorin Krenn

If you are genuinely happy with the relationship status of a situationship, by all means, stay there.

But if you know in your heart that you're only there because you're hoping they will one day want a committed relationship, then we must stop lying to ourselves and stand firm in our truth.

The greater the disconnect between what you truly want and what you are accepting, the more shame and lack of self-love you are building within yourself.

If someone has confirmed that they don't want a relationship through their words or actions, and yet you keep jumping through hoops to be available to them or to please them hoping they will change for you, then you are being toxic to yourself.

If you are dissatisfied with what you are getting in love and life, then you are responsible for changing that.

You can either honour and respect yourself and walk away from hot-cold, on-off dynamics, or you can continue hoping that your love will change the other person if you just keep hanging around.

Truth…

People change when they want to, not when you want them to.

People are ready for a relationship when they are, not when you need them to be.

It is their own desire, willingness and commitment towards change that changes them. And it could also be a reflection of how much they love and desire you.

Even if you are coming from a manipulative place, over-extending yourself and over functioning to keep the connection in your life it is actually the worst strategy that you could utilise to convert the other person into wanting you.

The chances of someone committing to you by you staying involved in a situationship with them is close to zero.

When they can have their cake and eat it too, what is the incentive for them to change? How will they miss you? See your full worth?

If there's anything that would inspire a change of heart

with someone, it would be the realisation that they risk losing you if they are unwilling to offer a relationship if that is what you seek.

Walk away from them, not because you want to manipulate them into wanting you but because you don't want to be in a misaligned connection that is born out of self-abandonment.

If you want a committed relationship, then honour that desire.

You deserve it.

AFFAIRS AND THIRD-PARTY SITUATIONS

An affair often wakes you up in such a way that you can't go back to sleep.

I have no judgement towards anyone who has had an affair.

I can't.

Many clients of mine were the individual who had an affair in their marriage. Just as many of my clients have experienced their spouse having an affair which ultimately ended their relationship.

I hear the pain, impact and turmoil that the presence of a third party has on everyone involved. Therefore, I can't have judgement.

The stereotype of men being the one to have more affairs is no longer true in this age.

Not everyone who had an affair is a horrible or selfish person.

Not everyone is moving forward thinking only with their libido.

I am not defending them.

I believe affairs are wrong and unkind to the other people in the relationship.

I believe them to be very wrong if you have an affair and are not honest and authentic with your partner about it. Horribly wrong if they are suspicious of a third-party presence in your relationship and to smooth things over you are downplaying their suspicion and intuition to hide your truth and behaviour.

That is cruel behaviour that no one deserves. To make someone doubt and question themselves and their intuition destroys a person's confidence and sense of self-trust. And you don't give them the opportunity to steer forward their own life, on their terms. You are interfering in their life path by withholding the full truth from them, deciding for them what they need to know or would benefit from knowing.

I know that my views on affairs might be hard to accept for those here who have been cheated on, who feel abandoned or wronged.

I ask you to see this from my perspective. I am privy to both sides of the story, often in more depth and having heard more honesty about people's truth and feelings than was ever expressed to their partner (usually as a way to avoid further hurting their partners or causing a bigger fallout).

This is not me justifying an affair or defending anyone.

I'm simply acknowledging that, for some, the affair is the soul's wakeup call that some need to have.

My personal values on relationships are always based on honesty and truth and I believe this should be the case for every relationship.

As soon as full honesty and transparency leaves a relationship, however someone tries to repair it or gloss over it, you have created discord in the relationship. Someone needs to shut down their intuition and not listen to it for the relationship to continue without discord.

People have affairs because their relationship is no longer meeting all of their needs, because it is no longer a reflection of who they are now or who they desire to be.

And people have affairs because they've overstayed in a relationship that doesn't meet their needs.

An affair wakes someone up to what they are missing and needing in an intimate relationship, whether it is an emotional or physical affair. These are often needs that an individual has been downplaying, abandoning and ignoring as necessary for their soul before the affair.

An affair doesn't have to be the end of your relationship if it's approached and talked about with transparency and full honesty from all parties. But it should be the opportunity for honesty and to reflect on what needs to change in the relationship. And if that change can even happen in this relationship.

Certainly, if you have been the victim of an affair or a third-party situation, I want you to know this, and as challenging an ask that this might be for you, please don't take an affair or their choice of person they had an affair with personally.

It is a reflection of their unmet needs that they were trying to meet and fulfil in another person. It is not a reflection of your shortcomings in any way.

They outgrew you. Perhaps for many years they could feel this happening and were trying to fight their feelings and continued to show up in the relationship because they did love and care for you, until one day they couldn't any longer.

We will never fully know.

What I hear over and over from those who have had an affair is:

I'm not this person.

I never meant for this to happen.

I feel so guilty.

What do I do now because I can't go back to how things were?

There are always two sides to every coin.

And while we can judge someone harshly for doing what they've done and for ending a relationship in this way, what I do wish for your soul? For you to not carry this forward in your heart and make it anything about you.

Instead, I'd like you to reflect and think, *I wish they'd had the courage to tell me that they were unhappy and weren't sure if they still wanted to be here with me for me. Not here because of our children and the home we'd built together. Regardless of everything, I wish they'd had the courage to be honest.*

Because all of us deserve to be in a relationship with someone who wants to be fully with us. For someone to be with us because they love us, not because they feel obliged to be with us or fear the financial, personal, or social fallout consequences of leaving us.

That's not love.

For many that's marriage.

ATTACHING TO NEW LOVE FAST

'Try not to confuse attachment with love. Attachment is about fear and dependency, and has more to do with love of self than love of another. Love without attachment is the purest love because it isn't about what others can give you because you're empty. It is about what you can give others because you're already full.'
— Yasmin Mogahed

Is this you?

This almost always occurs due to a perceived belief of their being a lack of love in the world for you. Finally, someone sees you and makes you feel appreciated. Offers love, affection and attention. We are hooked in with how it makes us feel about ourselves, we are excited by the potential we see in them, even though we don't really know them yet. We are attached.

We haven't even begun to fully know the individual.

Their ins and outs.

All of their personalities and qualities.

Their children and family dynamics.

Allowing love and a connection to grow slowly with someone is one of life's joys. A process of revealing yourself to someone over time and them to you. Magic upon magic that, with the right person, builds into a magnetic crescendo of attraction and connection with another. The energy is magnetic when we don't rush in and instead simply allow the process to unfold naturally in due course.

The energy becomes like an addiction when do you rush in. For good, bad or healthy, we're attached and hooked in. Blind to whether someone is aligned with our soul or not.

My biggest desire is for you to allow the time and space to let someone reveal themselves to you. Without any future thinking, imagining or projecting from you.

Simply you in the now, enjoying the process of getting to know someone in the now. Seeing them for who they are now.

I always ask my clients to allow three months to get to know a person as a mature adult. For all their nuances, desires and baggage. We all have these attributes!

Date as though love is everywhere around you, because it is.

Date as though you deserve only the best, because you do.

You have the power to choose who you love and attach too through the power and observance of your thoughts. Ask yourself: are you imagining too far ahead with this person after only one or two dates? (Even if it is amazing.)

Because you can very much desire to see a person again without being attached and pinning all your future dreams on to them as I see so many do.

I would love for you to date from a place of who you want to be with over who wants to be with you.

This is a very impactful, energetic shift that will raise your vibration from one of neediness to one of enjoying getting to know a person.

Love does not rush.

Only people do.

WHEN YOUR HEART HAS BEEN BROKEN TOO MANY TIMES

'Every relationship is a spiritual assignment and soul contract. So be grateful for the past. They may have broken you heart, but they also opened your eyes.'
— Mel Wells

When we leave a marriage there are three pathways a soul will take.

There is the pathway where someone has no desire to change or grow, maybe they see no need to, so they will dive straight into their next relationship. One that tends to be a shade of the same.

There is the pathway where someone is already in alignment with themselves, they know themselves well, they can also find themselves back in a relationship again relatively quickly. One that now matches their alignment and values.

Or there is the pathway where someone is quite out of alignment with themselves. They have not been living at their fullest expression or potential in the relationship and so their journey is to grow, to find themselves and to step into their fullest potential and expression. To find their alignment.

This latter person can often be left feeling like the journey to finding love is more of a battle-strewn path to walk.

They learn who they are and what they need now through the contrast of good and bad love and life experiences after leaving a marriage. They love only to outgrow because they are ascending in different ways all the time.

I know this person because I was this person.

This individual will grow more than most around them for a period of time. Becoming a completely new version over time. Because of this journey, they will also say the words at some point in time, 'I can't do love anymore, I'm tired of putting myself through it.'

When your heart has been hurt or disappointed too many times, I ask, please don't close, please just rest.

Please just take time out.

Please don't close your heart.

Take time to nurture you, not from a wounded space but from a place of self-care.

There is nothing in life worth closing our heart over.

Choosing to live with an open heart, no matter what life throws at us, is the ultimate self-mastery. And the only way we do this is to make the deliberate decision to not close and to stay open.

> 'There is a very simple method for staying open.
> You stay open by never closing.'
> — Michael A. Singer

Do not let anything in life be wounding enough that you close your heart over it. You can either close because you don't like what happened or you can choose to keep feeling love, hope, trust and enthusiasm despite it all.

Closing our heart does not really protect us from anything. Closing our hearts only serves to block us from being open to the things we actually desire to come in, which are love, connection, joy and enthusiasm.

Defining what we need to have in our life or what needs to show up in our life to be open in our hearts only limits us. We either open to all that life brings us despite it all, or we close to what life brings us.

I ask, please remain open to it all.

And choose to open to it again as soon as you can.

One day you will reach the space where you have entirely fallen out of the habit of closing your heart to protect yourself.

You are open and don't even realise that you are.

Watch your energy and life path shift to one of expansion as you continue to do this.

Just keep opening and opening again and not closing.

FEARING VULNERABILITY

'Being vulnerable is the only way to allow your heart to feel true pleasure.'
— Bob Marley

How do you stay open to love when you've been hurt before?

It takes tremendous courage to love with an open heart and to risk being hurt again. It's one of the scariest things we must move through after heartbreak.

We have to be willing to open ourselves to someone again. To allow them a place in our heart and in our world while knowing that they might leave us, hurt us or disappoint us along the way.

But what's the alternative of not being vulnerable and open hearted? To live life with a closed heart? To be emotionally unavailable, detached or closed to love? Never trusting again or never letting anyone in again for fear that you'll get hurt?

That, to me, is like having a car accident and then never driving again just in case you have another car accident one day.

Being vulnerable doesn't mean having zero boundaries. You can protect your heart while still remaining open, while still being cautious and highly selective about who you allow to take residence in your heart.

But boundaries are not armour.

If you recognise now that you perhaps have more armour on than you have healthy boundaries, then this is something to heal on your soul path.

Loving another and allowing another to fully love us requires us to have armour and shields down. This is how we open up to true intimacy.

As one of my clients said to me, 'I knew I had things backwards when I'd already had sex with him but was too shy and hesitant to reach out and hold his hand when we were walking the next day. Somehow reaching out to hold hands felt more intimate.'

Reflect on this for a moment.

IGNORING YOUR INTUITION TO STAY IN A RELATIONSHIP

Everyone talks about how hard it is to trust people after you've been hurt. But barely anyone talks about how hard it is to trust yourself when you've had your gut instincts and convictions skilfully undermined by someone.

Your intuition is your soul's magical power.

The inner knowing that doesn't always make sense but knows.

The sixth sense all of us have.

I hear this regularly from my clients when they are sharing with me the dynamics of their marriage—whether they're still in it or whether they've left.

- I knew something was going on. I suspected.
- I knew we shouldn't have married before we were married.
- They always turned it around on me like I was overthinking, anxious, reading too much into things. As though I was the problem.
- I started to believe I was insecure.
- It never felt right or added up to me and I couldn't ever let it go in my head or with him.
- I ignored my intuition. I listened to them more than I listened to myself.

Truth.

No amount of gaslighting, emotional manipulation,

control, attempts to forget or smoothing things over will shut down a person's intuition once it's been sparked.

Someone might try to ignore their intuition by choice or through persuasion, perhaps for many years to avoid the consequences of actually listening to it.

But once that antenna is on, it's on. And it will take only the slightest things in the future to flag it again and remind them.

The price an individual pays for ignoring their intuition or having their intuition downplayed as wrong when it's actually right, is high. In their loss of confidence, sense of self-worth, their sexual openness with their partner, their everything.

They will close off emotionally and sexually over time as a response.

When you are staying in a relationship that requires you to ignore or downplay your intuition, you are laying and have laid the blueprint for a disconnected relationship.

This is why someone can arrive at their late thirties, forties and fifties, and find themselves in a relationship that their younger, less wise, less confident self created the blueprint for. One that their older more evolved self can no longer tolerate.

The soul lesson here is the importance in trusting our intuition over ignoring it. Even if we don't know what has flagged our intuition exactly, simply admitting to ourselves that it is on and we don't know why is an important acknowledgement.

This needs to be enough to make us stop, listen, take off the rose-coloured glasses and reflect.

Our intuition is like a muscle. The more we trust it

and make decisions from that place, the more the muscle grows. The more confident we are making decisions from our intuition, more than our logic.

Intuition = voice of the soul.

Logic = voice of the ego and the human mind.

And just like the dissatisfaction of the soul, intuition can't be quietened for long.

BECOMING AN ENERGETIC MATCH FOR YOUR IDEAL PARTNER

'Too often we forget that an ideal partner is someone who enhances an already full existence.'
— Mariella Frostrup

What do you desire in a partner now?

As I've dated and left long-term relationships since my divorce, my ideal partner has changed. Things I believed were important that I needed in someone turned out to be not so important. And things that I thought weren't, all of a sudden became absolute non-negotiables.

I always ask my clients when they are open to love to write down a list of ideal qualities that they would love to have in a partner. We look at the physical attributes, the personality traits, children, family attitudes and lifestyle to really create a picture of how this person moves through the world and how they love.

And then I ask them this:

Who would your ideal partner be attracted to?

What is their type?

Knowing what we want in an ideal partner is a clarifying exercise and powerful manifesting technique but only if we come to it from a place of asking if we are an energetic match for them also.

Like attracts like.

Would they be attracted to us as we exist today?

Someone who is health conscious and exercises four to five times a week is more than likely also going to be attracted to a health-conscious person.

Someone who loves to be social and who enjoys the night life isn't going to be necessarily aligned with someone who never wants to go out.

I know this to be true for me. I very rarely drink. I actually can't remember the last time I was drunk or had a hangover. It was that many years ago. And so, I could never be in a relationship with someone who spent regular weekends hungover on the couch or smelling like alcohol next to me in bed.

This is no judgement to them or anyone who does this, it's merely a reflection of my values and ideal qualities in a person.

Sometimes the pathway to being in alignment so we run into and meet our ideal partner looks like us realising that if I like this type of characteristic in a person then maybe I need to embody even more of this in myself—in my energy, in my behaviour, in how I live my life.

This is us co-creating and becoming our own best version of self.

Which is also our ideal partner's ideal partner.

Some questions for you to ponder:

Am I this person already? Or am I waiting for their entry into my life to become this person?

FOR THOSE WHO ARE MORE COMFORTABLE GIVING LOVE THAN RECEIVING IT

Over-givers attract takers. And takers attract givers.

Like two pieces of a jigsaw puzzle that fit together perfectly. Notice how someone who loves to take more than they love to give never finds themselves in a relationship with someone who is also a taker? Why would they? For them there would be nothing attractive about that dynamic at all. Two takers in a relationship would butt heads, neither would feel loved, both claiming the other was selfish. A taker feels loved and nurtured when someone over-gives to them. An over-giver believes they have to over-give to be loved. See how perfectly these two fit together?

Both of these individuals more than likely learnt this way of loving from their parents during childhood. Maybe they watched one of their parents over-giving and loving the other in this way and have carried forth the behaviour into adulthood. Perhaps the taker was over-nurtured in their childhood by a parent, so this now forms their expectation of what love looks like.

If you are an over-giver then you probably feel exhausted and like no one gives to you. The cure? Stop over-giving. Recognise that love also looks like receiving love and nurturing from others. I'd love for you to start expecting this. Not because you're needy but because you're worthy of receiving love. And just like someone who is uncomfortable receiving compliments needs to learn to accept compliments comfortably without brushing them off, so do you need to learn to start receiving love by allowing space for it and accepting it when it is given to you.

You do not have to over-give to the point of self-sacrifice to be loved or to keep love in your life. This is not love. This is your conditioning and it is a karmic lesson of self-love and self-worth for you to evolve past.

PEOPLE-PLEASING AND THE DESIRE TO PLEASE

'Ironically, people-pleasing in order to keep a sense of belonging usually leads to the opposite outcome; feeling unseen and unappreciated.'
— Layne Beachley

A marriage ending is often the death of the people-pleaser. It's the death of conformity. Of tolerating mediocrity. Of being who others needed you to be. And you're wondering why it felt so hard to make a decision to leave your marriage and to have the courage to own it? An important reflection to see here is that people-pleasing adults were first people-pleasing children. Every time.

People-pleasing isn't inherently negative. All of us desire to please our loved ones. You might go out of your way to do things for the people in your life based on what you assume they want or need. You give up your time and energy to get them to like you.

But people-pleasing generally goes beyond simple kindness. It often involves changing or altering words, behaviours and our needs for the sake of another person's feelings or reactions or to keep them in our life.

This is how people-pleasing can cause trouble in our relationships. It becomes assumed that we will always put others before ourselves. We begin to feel unappreciated and taken advantage of. People-pleasers often deal with low self-worth and draw their self-worth by gaining approval and a sense of belonging from others. They desire others to like them and fear being rejected or ostracised for putting their needs above the needs of others first. People-pleasers tend to have very little spare time because they are giving to everyone else in their lives in their spare time.

Importantly, on our path to finding our one, we have to realise that our tendency to people-please will almost always attract into our life relationships that are not satisfying and that take advantage of us rather than celebrate us.

Practising putting yourself first and having boundaries and saying 'no' is how we slowly begin to overcome our people-pleasing tendencies over time. This almost always feels uncomfortable first because behaving in this way triggers our fears of belonging and of possible rejection.

Allow yourself to slowly expand into the energy of pleasing yourself first before others. Allow others to adjust to the new you who is beginning to say no, particularly if others are used to you always saying yes and dropping everything for them.

At first this might all feel selfish to you, but trust me when I say this, if you are a people-pleaser what you deem 'selfish' is usually far from it.

WE ALL DESERVE LOVE BUT SOME OF US ARE LESS READY THAN WE REALISE

'Be ready for love when it does come. Prepare the field and be ready to nourish love. Be loving, and you will be lovable. Be open and receptive to love.'
— Louise L. Hay

I talk to a lot of people who meet emotionally unavailable people. What many people don't see however is their own emotional unavailability playing out in the story. I wonder if you were completely open to love and ready to let someone into your life, you would have been attracted to them?

Most times if we look at an emotionally unavailable partner, we can see the ways in which their reluctance for a fully committed relationship in some ways kind of suited us and our lifestyle.

Perhaps we were more hesitant about love than we realised.

We feared rejection and vulnerability still.

Perhaps we were in the season of enjoying our independence and freedom.

Maybe we had very little spare time or energy left to truly offer a partner.

All I know is this because I see it time and time again: the more emotionally ready and open you are to love and to being in an actual relationship, the less attractive emotionally unavailable people become to you.

Their emotional unavailability and inconsistency becomes boring.

It becomes not enough.

It becomes hurtful and disappointing.

You lose interest over trying to keep their interest.

Make sure you aren't blinded by fear and pain from the past. Recognise that you too are perhaps a little more guarded and emotionally available than you realised. And unless two emotionally unavailable people are consciously aware about their unavailability and both working to heal it then we risk you becoming even more emotionally closed and unavailable because of the nature of the relationship.

Do the healing you need to do, knowing that time doesn't heal, it's what we do with the time that heals, so that you will be able to embrace what you deserve and move on from what is not that.

LEADING WITH APPEARANCES

Finding love after divorce is a soul journey. It is not an "I need to get a tighter booty, new wardrobe and a six pack" journey.

I see this regularly. We find ourselves single and one of the first things we do is turn our attention to looking good, losing weight and updating our wardrobe to attract our next partner.

Being attracted to someone is essential in an intimate, loving relationship. Without that energy, you are mere friends or acquaintances.

So, your looks, while not everything, are important.

Your partner must be attracted to you and vice versa.

However, when we lead with the way we look and our physical body as our leading asset... then both are a hindrance.

Many leave a long-term relationship because one of their biggest needs is to feel desired, to feel sexy again and for someone else to see and appreciate them for it.

This is when someone starts to lead with their looks and their physical form over and above their soul and what they have to give to a person from that level.

It's also the danger space where we can meet individuals who only see in us our physical looks and sex because they're leading with it too. As a result, we are going to attract those who are seeking mostly or only that.

The physical skin. Sex. To be desired. How a partner looks next to them.

Like attracts like.

If someone is leading with their physical attributes as their best asset, then they value it first and foremost too. They're more than likely going to see that in you too.

This is why some of the most beautiful of women can end up with some of the lousiest men who don't appreciate them as souls, as people. The women have learnt through life experience that their looks were vital to their success. The drawcard. And they define themselves by their physical appearance as a result.

Who do you think they attract? Men who choose them based more on their physical appearance and how they looked over genuine soul connection.

Inherently, this is two people coming from their humanness—from their ego.

I want someone to value you for who you are and your soul as much as how you look.

This means you have to value who you are and your soul first.

You have to be in touch with this side of yourself.

Let someone fall in love with that first.

Let who you are be the hook that captures them.

Not just how you look.

APPLYING RULES OF RIGHT AND WRONG TO LOVE

If love did come with a rule book, throw it out.

I can't believe he did that.

I can't believe she did that.

That's so wrong.

We hear these kinds of sentiments spoken a lot about love and relationships. I'm not defending bad behaviour at all but... love has no rules.

Someone will leave your life for one reason only to come back better for the time apart, now ready and knowing what they want. And someone can do the complete opposite. They leave. They wake up. They stay gone.

You can be comfortably married to someone. Happily settled with your future fate and yet you connect eyes with someone unexpected and they cause an awakening and everything changes for you. There are some who might say they should never have pursued each other or they should have handled it differently, or not done this or that but I simply want you to recognise this.

There are no rules in love.

Love and connections just show up in life. Usually when we're not looking for it. Rules don't apply to love as much as we try to make them fit. When it comes to the presence of love in our life or the absence of it when someone leaves our life, we can only offer it two things: acceptance because we can't control the emotion of love in ourselves, certainly not in others; and detachment because we can't make someone love us and be ready for us when they aren't.

Love has no rules. But the journey does always make sense in the end.

You never know what is right around the corner or what life is preparing you for during your soul life path. Life could be orchestrating your wildest dreams to come to fruition and it will blow you away.

Stay humble, grounded and keep trusting.

UNDERSTANDING THE FEMININE AND MASCULINE IN LOVE

'You and your man are either evoking in each other openness or closure, worship or distance.'
— David Deida

If we are to look at the masculine energy in a love relationship, what is it?

The masculine exists as the container to the feminine who is held, loved and supported within it. In an ideal relationship with beautiful polarity this is the balance.

The masculine is the container.

The feminine exists within it.

In an off-balance relationship, we can see the opposite. Instead, the feminine is the container carrying and driving the relationship. Holding it together. And the masculine exists within the container, taking an almost back seat in the relationship, keeping the peace, going with her flow more often than not.

In this relationship we see the feminine person in the relationship more in her masculine energy, the one in control and often feeling resentful and tired as a result of it but feeling safe because she is in control—which is what she ultimately needs and desires.

And we see the masculine person in this relationship more in his feminine energy by consequence and feeling like he has little to no freedom, slightly emasculated, slightly resentful as a result of it, but feeling cared for and nurtured. This person bites their tongue to keep the peace.

They dismiss and downplay their needs.

In a less-than-trustworthy, committed energy we see this analogy of a container felt by the feminine. Her intuition picking up on the leaky energy of the container of the relationship that she is in when she feels her partner is sharing his energy or attention in anyway with other women.

For the premise of your own soul journey through love there are several questions to ask ourselves here.

In past relationships have you been the container or in the container? Was that aligned with your natural energy of being either feminine or masculine?

If you are the masculine energy, it is to ask ourselves, *When I have been in a relationship how solid, strong and nurturing has the container been that I provided to my partner? Was it of quality?*

If the masculine doesn't like the results that he has received in love in the past then this is the question he must ask himself that empowers him to love better and do better. And to choose a partner who respects the container if he knows he is producing one of quality.

And if we are the feminine energy it is to ask ourselves the opposite. *In past relationships what has been the quality of container that I have placed myself in? Have they been loving, supportive, caring, nurturing and safe for me? Have I trusted it?*

If the feminine doesn't like the results that she has received in love in the past then this is the question she must ask herself that empowers her to make a better choice in who she entrusts herself with. She must also acknowledge the importance of trusting her intuition if she feels the leaky energy of a container.

Generationally and culturally, we have much to do around allowing and empowering men to be in their masculine energy. Certainly, what many see as strong masculine energy today is far from what it really is at its core.

Many women are also more in their masculine energy then they realise. They are the container in the relationship. Certainly, it is something I 'treat' with almost every female client that I work with to varying degrees. Our culture of striving and success, resentment built up from carrying the energetic burden of children and relationships, and a fear of vulnerability after heartbreak or hurt shifts the feminine very quickly into a more masculine closed, protective energy.

The feminine doesn't tell the masculine what to do. Instead, she gracefully influences him, often this looks like expressing her needs and holding him accountable. He can do whatever he wants. But she won't tolerate everything.

In the former you sound like his mum. In the latter you are a sovereign, powerful, magnetic being.

Feel the difference?

As a result of so many men not being in their masculine—strong, grounded, true to their word and in their purpose and as a result of so many women not being in their feminine—loving, nurturing, more going with the flow, soft, playful, confident, is why we are seeing such a discord in so many relationships and the dating pool today.

We are absolutely seeing a rebalancing of masculine and feminine energies in relationships and within ourselves in this generational moment of time.

Women expecting better quality containers of relationships to be in otherwise they will leave. Why be in something if you don't have to be and put yourself through it? The toxic, manipulative, lying and cheating behaviour is less and less accepted.

Men who have done the work who need women to energetically step down and allow them to be in their masculinity and to be that container for them.

The power always returning to the feminine. If you don't like the quality of the container that you find yourself in, then don't be in it.

Do you know what really weakens a man?

Porn.

Scrolling on socials.

Prioritising making money.

Video games.

Drugs and alcohol.

Being in a relationship with a woman who is guarded, emotionally and sexually closed and controlling also contributes further to their emasculation.

A weakened man looks for a woman to lead him and give him direction because he doesn't know how to do that for himself.

A strong, healthy man has boundaries, purpose, clear direction, a relationship that nourishes his masculine energy and he is grounded.

Do you know what really wounds a woman?

Hustle culture.

Needing to feel in control.

Ignoring their intuition.

Replacing feelings with logic.

Abandoning playfulness for seriousness.

Not trusting the masculine and being in relationships where she doesn't trust him and intuitively feels his leaky energy, but ignores and downplays it.

A wounded woman seeks to control and curtail the freedoms of the man in her life because she fears being hurt and can feel the leaks.

An at-peace, relaxed sensual woman leads with her intuition and her feelings and makes her decisions from this place. She opens and shares herself where she knows she will be loved well. She is a beautiful mix of soft and strong. She is wise as much as she is playful.

It will take time but as women reconnect to their feminine essence and men become more rooted in their strong masculinity, then love and relationships will heal and ascend.

This is the soul work for all of us as we look to find love and our one after divorce.

For women to only place themselves in masculine containers that support them to be in their feminine and at their best essence. For men to be of the energy necessary to be these strong containers and to choose to be in relationships with women that have the awareness to nourish this in them.

FEELING DISHEARTENED WHILE ON THE LOVE JOURNEY

Synchronicity and divine timing is the universe's way of seducing you. Because it wants to lead you somewhere. It wants to bring you to the ultimate experience of being yourself and loving yourself.

I can't keep putting myself out there anymore.

When will love happen for me?

I'm tired of doing life on my own.

These are common sentiments I hear expressed from men and women who are waiting for life to bring them their one—or sometimes just a *someone*. What I am about to say next may disappoint you.

Life is more than just about whether you have a relationship in your life or not. Which doesn't mean you can't have moments of feeling disheartened or moments of 'I wish…' or 'when will they show up?' But it does mean that we must keep living and enjoying our life to the fullest in the meantime and to enjoy the process of doing everything else we were meant to experience along the way.

Synchronicity and divine timing.

These are beautiful energies. They also create magical stories of love just arriving one day and walking into our life with ease, feeling like it was meant to be and at the perfect time.

This will absolutely happen for you.

I would like to suggest that there might be a reason why love hasn't happened for you yet. I hope this book has revealed to you something about that.

What I will say is to please never allow your moments of feeling disheartened to lead you to settle or compromise in love. Always remind yourself that your life is better enjoyed when you're happily single and loving life over being in a relationship for the sake of it.

Everything you desire is out there waiting for you and all it is needing from you is for you to be living as the person that you always were underneath—you in your soul alignment.

Love will struggle to find you and stay in your life when you embody the energy of someone who sits at home depressed on the couch.

Thrive in life.

Work hard to be your best version of self.

Trust the process.

Stay grounded.

Seek meaningful connections and hobbies you love.

Surround yourself with good people.

Expand your world and your horizons.

Let the one find you. Let yourself accidentally stumble across love instead of always searching for it.

PART 5

Guidance to Help You on Your Journey to Finding the One

A BIRD'S-EYE VIEW OF YOU: WHAT IS YOUR CURRENT LIFE PATH HURDLE?

'I'm in between a life that's ending, that used to be a certain way, and a new one that's beginning, but I don't see clearly ahead of me where I end up … so what do you do? You don't stop in the fog. You just keep moving one step at a time, and trust that wherever this leg of the journey is taking you, its' where you were meant to be.'
— Mel Robbins

I want you to take finding love off your life path for a moment. Take it completely off. We're doing this because it's not ours to put on.

Love shows up when it's meant to.

Love shows up when it will.

Love just shows up when you're happily doing your thing.

We have control over many things in our life. But not love.

If we remove love from your life path, what can we see is your current life path hurdle? What can you see yourself needing to focus on or overcome right now? This is a beautiful clarifying question for us to use when we are over-focusing on the lack of relationship in our life.

As if the presence of love in our life fixes and absolves us from everything else.

It does not.

This is not the ideal attitude or energy to have about love.

I'm not asking you to close yourself off to finding love by viewing your life path in this way. I'm asking you to instead be open to love showing up for you while you are mastering and living your life as your best version of self in the now.

To be ascending in your own soul growth, healing and evolvement. Moving forward towards your one. Not standing on the spot, as the same version of self you've always been, waiting for them.

What is it that you need to master and overcome in the now?

THE TAO: FINDING YOUR OWN INNER BALANCE AND PATH TO YOUR ALIGNMENT

'The Tao is in the middle. It's where energy is not pushing in either direction. The pendulum will come to a balance in all areas of life, if we allow it, because everything has its own yin and yang. The Way is where these forces quietly balance.'
— Michael A. Singer

The Tao.

The way.

The balance of the yin and the yang.

The feminine and the masculine.

The dark and the light.

The fine balance that exists between the two extremes of cup so full and cup so empty.

Let us use the example of hunger to best explain the Tao. What is the saying? A human is only nine meals away from anarchy! Imagine yourself having gone without nine straight meals over several days. Imagine how hungry you would feel (one extreme) and imagine how you would react when you were finally given food to eat.

Starving so much that you would find yourself eating so quickly, overeating. Now feeling so full, satisfied but also a little uncomfortable (the other extreme).

The Tao exists between both those extremes where the energies are balanced. A place of neither being so uncomfortably hungry or uncomfortably full.

The way of the centre is where we find balance and where we live in harmony.

When we participate and stay stuck in the extremes of anything is where we lose our way and waste our energy.

I see this in many clients after they leave a marriage. The marriage lacked sex, intimacy and attention (cup empty: extreme) so they enter into the dating world seeking connections that make them feel desired and sexy (cup full and overflowing: extreme).

Individuals in this example do this dance until the extreme starts to feel lonely, tiring and no longer fulfilling. In fact, it starts to make them feel unhappy too because it lacks the one element we seek inherently—soul connection.

Life begins to feel confused when we live in the place of extremes. Not because we are confused but because we're making life confusing through our behaviours.

From one extreme to the other, stopping only once we let go of the extremes and allow the energy in between both to settle and find balance. The energy of balance eventually permeating and entering into our psyche and our life.

When we come to love from a place of extreme, whether it is an emotional void or a sexual need, we are actually coming to love from a place of being out of balance.

Sometimes we can reach this place of balance within a new relationship, which is of course ideal when we do. Sometimes it can take several relationships or situationships for us to recognise we are coming from a place of extreme and to clear it from our system.

A few things to be aware of when we are looking for love after divorce:

In what way am I out of balance?

What am I really seeking here?

Am I in balance or out?

Is what I am doing good for me in my attempts to correct my lack of balance?

In what way is the individual we are dating or in a relationship with out of balance?

As you centre by not participating in the extremes, this is when the energies within you will naturally find their balance.

Find your balance between the extremes and you will find yourself in growing harmony with your soul alignment.

You will find yourself on your path.

BRINGING TO LIFE YOUR BEST-CASE SCENARIO AND NOT YOUR WORST!

'It's already yours.'
— Universe

Almost everyone I ask can tell me their fears and their worst-case scenarios without having to give too much thought to their answer. Very few can give me their best-case scenario that they'd love to see for themselves in the next six months, one year, five years or the rest of their life with the same ease. Without realising, most of us are predominately thinking about what we don't want and what we fear more than what we do want. No wonder you are co-creating and manifesting into your life everything you don't want and not what you do want.

Look at all that you're focusing on!

When I can switch my clients' thought process to be predominantly focused on their best-case scenario without attachment to a particular person, place or thing instead of their worst-case scenario is when we create magic in their lives. We focus on what we do want. We release our attachment to certain people needing to be the person to instrument our best-case scenarios coming to life. We place ourselves on the path of finding our soul alignment and we let everything that is an energetic match to our best-case scenario come to us and we let everything fall away that is not.

The best-case scenario for ourselves becomes the intention.

It is a powerful practice and manifesting technique.

Try it.

Write your best scenario down. Vision board it if you desire. Visit it regularly as a reminder every time you feel waylaid or find your thinking is trying to lead you back to the safety and comfort of expecting the worst.

Expecting and thinking about the worst-case scenario is a habit.

Change the habit.

Prepare for the best to walk into your life instead.

WHAT DOES THIS PERSON BRING OUT IN ME? THE BEST AND THE WORST

'The right people will always bring out the best parts of you. They will bring out the sun and watch you bloom.'
— R.M. Drake

We can love someone deeply and they can still not be good for us. Freedom and peace is accepting someone for who they are and not needing them to be anyone else, or any different to who they are now. Freedom and peace is also not fighting someone on this and releasing yourself from a situation that isn't bringing out the best in you or the connection. Freedom and peace is also owning what you do need.

It is important to acknowledge when someone is truly

not good for us or bringing out the best in us.

Placing myself in positive relationships and environments for work and love has completely changed my life. People who want the best for you and support you by giving you their best self, not only change your outlook on life but also your sense of self. You will go from feeling like you're too much or not enough to realising you are just perfect and loved as you are.

Go where you feel appreciated and are supported to shine, grow and evolve.

IF I LET GO OF MY ATTACHMENT TO THIS ONE PERSON WHAT CAN I SEE THIS LOVE IS TRYING TO TEACH ME?

'Learn the difference between connection and attachment. Connection gives you power, attachment sucks the life out of you.'
— Unknown

If we view love from a place of ascension and growth without attachment to a person, we open ourselves to seeing more clearly why they entered our life. Sometimes even why they had to leave.

Why did this person come into my life?

What did this person gift to me?

What did this person teach me about love?

What did they teach me about myself?

What did they bring out in me that I now see is

important and something I will take forward with me?

What was the lesson I needed to learn here?

And have I learnt it yet?

These are great journaling questions to ask yourself if you find yourself attached to a love that perhaps isn't bringing out the best in you and is more of a soulmate or karmic love.

Every lesson learnt in love carries us forward on our soul life path. Closer to being in our fullest expression and in alignment with ourselves.

Nearer to our one.

But more importantly, ready for them.

WHAT WAS IT ABOUT THEM THAT MADE ME LOVE BEING AROUND THEM?

'Check all your relationships. Many are attachments you created to fill a void in your soul left by low self-esteem, lust, fear and loneliness. Not all relationships in your life belong there. Some are just replacing the love that you haven't been giving to yourself.'
— Unknown

When we fall in love with, are we actually falling in love with is the feeling that they are bringing out in us and the way they make us feel about ourselves. Yes, we are still in love with the person and their qualities, but it is the mutual energy of the two of you together when you are connecting that is pulling at your soul and psyche.

Sometimes it is also what they open up within you. Allowing you to express and step into embodying a more brilliant version of yourself as a result of their love, attention and gaze, and loving you for it.

When a love leaves our life, whether this person returns to our life in time or not, this is the powerful reflection for us to have.

What was it about them that made me love being around them?

What did they bring out in me?

How did I feel about myself when I was with them?

The answers to these questions reveal the voids we can look to work on along our soul path. If someone made you feel sexy and desirable, can we not feel that way still without someone having to see that in us first? If they made you feel confident and good enough, can we not feel those things without someone choosing us and propping us up in those areas of self?

The difference between a karmic love, the loves that we so easily find ourselves stuck in and repeating, and a higher love connection like a twin flame connection?

Karmic soulmates are attracted to you when you're in a low vibration.

Twin flames are attracted to you when you're in a high vibration or on the pathway to being so. Not perfectly healed or in alignment, but on the pathway to.

Some of the greatest healing that we will go through is within these twin flame connections when they finally come into union in our life. When they go through the contrast of all of the stages of running, separation and coming together to clear our last final blocks and wounds away.

The more we step into this higher vibration, the closer we move towards being ready for those beautiful higher connections to come into our life and to stay in our life.

Not because they are karmic and oh so close but because they are our twin flame.

PART 6

A Letter to My Future Self and a Letter to Yours

A letter to my future self.
A letter to yours.

Opening to the unknown.
To becoming a version of self that I felt was possible and
wanted to explore.
Vibrant.
Alive.
On fire.
Loving.

I released all versions of who I was to arrive to her.
The stay-at-home mum—for a season.
The woman in a marriage she chose for herself in her
twenties—for a season.
The woman who lived for her children—for a season.
The woman who needed a man and his love to define
her—for a season.

I released her.
Reimagining me.
Reimagining who I am and who I was meant to be.

That has been the magical gift of my divorce.
The opportunity and the freedom to do so.
And the invitation for you to do the same.

Sometimes I think about what it would look like and how it would feel to have all my lovers of the past in one room. And to gaze over them with the wisdom of my eyes today.

This one taught me this.
This one taught me that.

To see them for the souls they were.
And the soul I was when I was with them.
The lessons they taught me.
The gift of their presence for a time in my world.
To stand in front of them all as the woman I am today, with all of my soul.

And say, thank you.
For bringing everything out in me that I am able to be today.
My highest identity and soul potential you helped awaken and create within me.

For the love, thank you.
For the hurt, thank you.

I took everything you gave me, and I turned it into something wonderful.
My soul assignment: to become the woman that I am today.

From the bottom of my heart,
Thank you.

Acknowledgements

I would like to express my deepest gratitude to the many, many women, in numbers that I don't know anymore, who have come to me as a client and trusted me to support them through this season of their lives. Sharing with me their inner turmoil, their emotions and the challenges they are struggling to move through. Your experiences, along with my own, allowed me to see the similar thought patterns within us all. And in the work of understanding humans, the ability to have pattern recognition is everything.

Your vulnerability with me has given me the strength to continue to be the voice for divorced and I-wish-I-could-leave-and-get-a-divorce people. As my work continues to ruffle a few feathers with the 'happily' married, it is your voice in my emails and DMs on social media that remind me always that the divorced, wishing-I-could-get-a-divorce and the truly happily married person actually deeply resonate and agree with my work. Therefore, I will continue to work and write for you knowing that I intend only the greatest, highest good for all.

Personally, I would like to acknowledge and thank the many beautiful humans in my life who have supported me to reach this place both personally and professionally in myself. The smallest of paragraphs here cannot convey to you my gratitude for your part in my evolvement and waking up. Whether small or large, every little piece has come together to bring me to where I am today.

I would also like to thank my publisher Natasha Gilmour for allowing me the creative and professional licence in both of my books to write on this topic of love and divorce and to share my views. Divorce and marriage is a highly triggering topic for many that is always going to illicit a strong response from some. I have always comfortably embraced this because my desire has always been to change the conversation around divorce to be one that is more positive-focused. Thank you, by osmosis, for doing this too.

Resources

Cynthia Hickman, *Handbook For Being Human*

Courtney Hunt, M.D., *Your Spark Is Light: The Quantum Mechanics of Human Creation*

Michael A. Singer, *The Untethered Soul*

Kate Rose, *You Only Fall in Love Three Times*

Leslie Sampson, *Find Your Twin Flame*

About the Author

CARLA DA COSTA is a divorce coach and author of *Seconds Please*, one of Australia's most-loved books on the subject of marriage dissolution. Carla has become a modern voice on marriage separation for women and men, and asks readers, is divorce truly a failure or could this be the best catalyst for change that has ever happened to you?

Through her private coaching practice, online programs and books, Carla works with people who are separated, divorced or divorcing, guiding them through these transformative experiences. Carla's practice supports and inspires women and men to make this next season of their life the best season of their life.

carladacosta.com
Facebook.com/carladacostaperth
Instagram: @carla_dacosta